# Learning Communities in Educational Partnerships

To Étienne,
With our very best wishes,

Máirín Glenn,
Mary Roche,
Bernie Sullivan
Caitríona McDonagh

## ALSO AVAILABLE FROM BLOOMSBURY

*Effective Action Research*, Patrick J. M. Costello
*Place-Based Methods for Researching Schools*, Pat Thomson
and Christine Hall
*Engaging with Educational Change*, Alma Fleet, Katey De Gioia
and Catherine Patterson
*Reflective Teaching in Schools*, Andrew Pollard
*Inquiring in the Classroom*, edited by Nick Mitchell and Joanne Pearson

# Learning Communities in Educational Partnerships

Action Research as Transformation

**MÁIRÍN GLENN, MARY ROCHE, CAITRIONA MCDONAGH AND BERNIE SULLIVAN**

Bloomsbury Academic
An imprint of Bloomsbury Publishing Plc

B L O O M S B U R Y

LONDON · OXFORD · NEW YORK · NEW DELHI · SYDNEY

**Bloomsbury Academic**
An imprint of Bloomsbury Publishing Plc

| 50 Bedford Square | 1385 Broadway |
| London | New York |
| WC1B 3DP | NY 10018 |
| UK | USA |

**www.bloomsbury.com**

**BLOOMSBURY and the Diana logo are trademarks of Bloomsbury Publishing Plc**

First published 2017

**British Library Cataloguing-in-Publication Data**
A catalogue record for this book is available from the British Library.

ISBN: HB: 978-1-4742-4356-8
PB: 978-1-4742-4357-5
ePDF: 978-1-4742-4359-9
ePub: 978-1-4742-4358-2

**Library of Congress Cataloging-in-Publication Data**
Names: Glenn, Máirín, author.
Title: Learning communities in educational partnerships :
action research as transformation / Máirín Glenn, Mary Roche,
Caitriona McDonagh and Bernie Sullivan.
Description: London, UK ; New York, NY, USA : Bloomsbury Academic, [2017] |
Includes bibliographical references and index. Identifiers: LCCN 2017004464 |
ISBN 9781474243568 (hb) | ISBN 9781474243575 (pb) |
ISBN 9781474243599 (ePDF) | ISBN 9781474243582 (ePub)
Subjects: LCSH: Professional learning communities. |
Action research in education. | Interdisciplinary approach in education.
Classification: LCC LB1731 .G559 2017 | DDC 370.71/1–dc23
LC record available at https://lccn.loc.gov/2017004464

Cover design by Olivia D'Cruz
Cover image © Getty Images/James Brey

Typeset by Newgen Knowledge Works (P) Ltd., Chennai, India
Printed and bound in Great Britain

To find out more about our authors and books visit www.bloomsbury.com.
Here you will find extracts, author interviews, details of forthcoming events
and the option to sign up for our newsletters.

# Contents

# Foreword

It is a story that needs to be told, and retold, across times and places.

Teachers coming together because they care deeply about the awesome responsibility they have accepted.

I have a confession to make. Even though I have spent my working life as a learning theorist, I am not sure I could be a teacher. What kind of human wizardry does it take to ensure that a classroom full of youngsters learn what they need to learn to become adults ready for a world we can't even imagine? It's this thing about practice that no amount of book writing or reading gives you. But if I was a teacher, I sure would want to spend time with my colleagues – reflecting, researching, inspecting, questioning, pushing the frontier and plumbing the depth, getting any help I can get.

So I really appreciate stories about social spaces where teachers reaffirm and nurture their commitment to the difficult art of teaching: where they focus on their vocation in a reflective mode, both celebrating and challenging their professional practice and identity. In these spaces, reflection brings theory and practice in lived interplay, theory informing practice, practice turning into theory.

The communities the authors describe are not created via top-down mandates. Teachers are coming together in their own time, on their own terms. This reveals their passion and their enthusiasm for learning together, for their benefit and for the benefit of those they serve.

In the context of school systems, this brings up an interesting question. If these conversations are so important to these teachers' professional capability and identity, shouldn't the institutions that employ them value these spaces and make them part of their work time? Or are these institutions incapable of supporting these spaces without undermining the very autonomy and inspiration that makes them valuable?

I do not know the full answer, but I do know that finding any kind of answer will depend on telling the story, on understanding better how these spaces function in the lives of dedicated professionals, when they have a chance to be agents of their learning.

Etienne Wenger-Trayner
October 2016

# Acknowledgements

This book is dedicated to everyone who, with wholeheartedness and openness of mind, seeks to improve their practice through participating in learning communities.

We would like to thank

- those who walked the initial steps with us as we experienced the benefits of a learning community, including our PhD tutor and colleagues in the Department of Education and Professional Studies in the University of Limerick 2001–2007

- the Teaching Council of Ireland, which commissioned our initial research into Continuous Professional Development for teachers

- all who have engaged in learning communities with us since 2007 and who enlightened us through their dialogue and critical engagement

- the editorial staff at Bloomsbury, who provided support and expertise in the lead-up to the publication of our book

- Dr Etienne Wenger-Trayner, who took time out from his busy schedule to pen the Foreword to this book.

# Glossary

**Cooperating teacher** the teacher in whose class/es a student teacher is placed while on practicum

**Educational values** beliefs around education and guiding principles that frame our teaching and learning. They underpin everyday practice

**Emancipatory practice** a form of practice grounded in freedom and empowerment

**Epistemological values** beliefs one holds about knowledge acquisition and generation

**Gaeilge** the Irish language

**Hegemonic** a system based on hierarchical order, where those at the top hold all the power over acquiescent, uncritical others

**Hybrid spaces** where two different perspectives might be accommodated in a non-antagonistic manner

**ITE or initial teacher education** a course of study for a student teacher

**Living contradiction** the holding of values but denying them in practice, a term developed by Jack Whitehead (see www. actionresearch.net)

**Living theory** a form of action research promoted by Jack Whitehead (see www. actionresearch.net)

**Non-synchronous or asynchronous** not occurring at the same time

**Ontological values** beliefs about our being in the world, our sense of self and how we relate to others

**Professional development, continuous professional development** and **professional learning** terms used interchangeably to mean the growth of one's professional knowledge, skills and dispositions

**Professional learning groups** or **professional learning community** groups of practitioners coming together with the shared purpose of improving their practice through action research

**School Head** also known as the School Principal or Head Teacher

**School placement, practicum, or teaching practice** teaching experience for student teachers in a school setting

**Self-study action research** a values-based enquiry into one's own practice using an action research approach

# Introduction

This book is an unfolding story. We authors are in the process of learning about learning communities and action research, and learning through them. We have not reached an 'end point' in our thinking, but we have spent nearly two decades negotiating with our own learning and the learning of others within learning communities, as well as engaging with the processes of self-study action research. Drawing on these experiences, we share the story of our learning and how we enable ourselves and others to work towards better practice, to generate theory from that new understanding and to potentially influence policy. Our book addresses the growing trend in educational contexts for teachers to participate in various educational partnerships often for evaluation purposes – with colleagues, with school leaders, with teacher education colleges, with student teachers, and with teachers in the early stages of their career (England, Department for Education 2012; Ireland, Department of Education 2016a, 2016b; Northern Ireland, Department of Education 2010; Scottish Executive 2005; The Teaching Council of Ireland, 2017). These partnerships have greatest influence when the participants form a learning community – a partnership in action.

A learning community, as we understand it, can provide an environment wherein participants may discover a capacity for intercommunication with fellow members of the community. They can develop the ability to carry on a dialogue with others, as they share their views, listen to, and respect their opinions. In the process, they begin to participate in the sharing of certain values and ideals that are important to the community and that characterize the interactions of its members. Members of a learning community need to feel safe when discussing their ideas, and need to feel that their individual contributions are respected, valued and appreciated. The term 'community' suggests a coming-together, a union or a merging that conjures up descriptors such as cooperation, sharing and collaboration – all positive attributes that can engender a sense of well-being and achievement. When we designate the community as a learning community, we are adding another dimension of positivity and possibility to the concept. The space that we create within our practice for sharing ideas, and inviting critique of our ideas, can result in new learning and new knowledge about our practice. The new knowledge thus created has the potential to achieve improvement and transformation of our educational practice.

The book is a collaborative undertaking, written by teachers, and is intended as a guide for teachers and student teachers, both practitioners and postgraduate researchers, and those who wish to personalize their learning within effective education partnerships. It is informative for teacher educators seeking ways of making critical reflection part of the school placement practicum. It provides a useful scaffold to cooperating teachers and mentors within the school placement setting. It guides practitioners working towards formal accreditation, as it offers explanations of the philosophical and theoretical basis of learning partnerships and communities. We authors show how our learning journeys can provide the inspiration for other teachers to form similar educational partnerships and enhance their professional development.

# Why we wrote this book

Convinced of the potential of self-study action research as an effective approach to professional development, we authors wished to encourage other educators to explore the possibility of using this approach. From 2010 to 2012 we established learning communities in various contexts to research the design of a new form of teacher Continuing Professional Development (CPD) based on our own experiences with self-study action research. The results were overwhelmingly positive. This book examines the process from both the authors' and participants' perspectives: it outlines the authors' journeys, the difficulties that arose for them and their learning from the research. It also describes some of the experiences of the educators who became involved in those learning communities – how they managed to improve their everyday work practices, their understanding of their practice and the subsequent learning that emerged for them in the process. We authors are convinced that, dealing as it does with the day-to-day challenges and difficulties of conducting self-study action research, the book will appeal to everyone wishing to adopt this approach to educational research.

Throughout the book, we use a self-study action research approach because of its relevance to understanding and improvement of practice, its potential for becoming a way of being that leads to enhanced professional development and its legitimacy in gaining formal academic accreditation. Grounded in constructivist principles of knowledge that accept that our learning is always in a process of becoming, we show how meaningful change can take place when educators are encouraged to draw on their own personal educational values and share their ideas in a community. At a practical level, we are showing how we established learning communities and how co-learners in our learning communities demonstrated that educators can be autonomous and are able to take charge of their own professional development in a positive and productive manner. We are recommending that others involved in educational partnerships would try similar approaches to their professional development. We are developing personalized theory from practice within educational learning communities, as we show how we have made spaces for professional conversations and effective communication.

We believe that the provision of a collegial space for teachers of all ages and experience to discuss and reflect collectively, as they support their own and others' individual practitioner enquiry projects, is professionally beneficial across the continuum precisely because each age/experience group has something of value to add to the conversation. Within this inclusive approach lies an inherent equality, where the contributions of all participants carry equal weight, and hierarchical issues are not a barrier to progress. Teachers, like all other professionals, need time and space for critical and constructive professional conversation. They need time to think about and discuss the kind of world and society they want for themselves and their children. Along with time and space in which to reflect on and develop their epistemological values about knowledge, knowing and knowers, teachers also need encouragement to identify and name their core ontological educational values so that they can hold their pedagogies up to scrutiny against these values to see if they are being realized. We authors believe that teachers are professionals who need to examine their practice through critical reflection, in order to see if it is caring and humane, inclusive and welcoming of diversity. We believe, too, that all who work in the service of others need to check if their ontological values are denying or supporting the building of a caring and democratic society. If not, then they need time to work out how they might go about improving the situation. However, as Palmer (1997: 11) pointed out, such opportunities are almost non-existent: 'We rarely talk with each other about teaching at any depth.'

When we argue throughout this book for teachers to engage in professional conversation, we are not just referring to the sharing of tips and tricks to help us get by day-to-day in a busy classroom – although this is valuable – we are looking at a much bigger picture that involves improvement and transformation. The alternative is an unexamined professional life. Over twenty years ago, Brookfield (1995) outlined the benefits of critical reflection for examining one's professional life. These were to do with the ability to provide a rationale for one's practice, professional self-awareness and the creation of democratic classrooms. Schools, however, are hectic spaces of activity. Dadds's (2001) hurry-along curriculum has not abated: it has intensified, if anything. In such busy institutional contexts, whether nursery school or university, finding time to reflect critically about shared values in a meaningful and authentic way can be difficult. If, as Clark (2001) says, teacher talk can be a potent medium for teacher learning and professional development, then it stands to reason that teachers need properly structured opportunities and spaces to support each other in such professional deliberations. In the foreword to this book, Wenger-Trayner asks if teacher employers should perhaps value these spaces and make them part of their everyday work.

# Organization of the book

For a number of years, we authors Máirín Glenn, Mary Roche, Caitriona McDonagh and Bernie Sullivan, have convened groups of educators from a broad spectrum of settings and introduced them to the underpinning ideas around self-study action research – a form of action research which, we explain, is supportive of, and conducive to, transformation. We provided a space for professional conversations, as well as scaffolding for the participating educators as they interrogated the assumptions underpinning self-study action research and carried out their personal research in their classroom situations. We see both of these forms of support as crucial to those undertaking endeavours aimed at improving practice. We also perceive such work to be predominantly process oriented rather than product oriented.

The educational partnerships, which we describe, moved away from the dominant form of CPD – which was, and still is, a more skills-based, 'one-shot, knowledge transfer model' (Conway et al. 2009: 187) – towards a model which acknowledges the idea that teachers are capable of making judgements about their own professionalism. Drawing on the notion of 'teacher as theorist' (Kadi-Hanifi 2010; Pockett and Giles 2008; Whitehead and McNiff 2006), the book offers a form of support that encourages educators to develop their own educational theories from their practice. They have been supported in their research by belonging to a community of teachers sharing in 'professional conversations' (Clark 2001). Our practical examples are classroom-based, focusing on the immediate educational concerns of teachers with the aim initially of improving practice and developing educational theory, and, possibly, of gaining postgraduate accreditation. In some cases, entire school staffs worked together and chose areas for improvement – at individual classroom levels. The projects were grounded in teacher self-evaluation.

The book focuses on various educational partnerships in which teachers may participate. In each chapter, reflective questions are offered as guides to readers who may wish to develop learning communities within educational partnerships. We have changed the names of participants throughout the book. Here is a synopsis of what readers may expect to encounter in the individual chapters as they progress through the book:

## Chapter 1 A Professional Learning Partnership

This chapter begins by describing how we established ourselves as a small learning community who wished to explore self-study action research as practitioner researchers. It explains how we wanted to extend our learning so as to enhance our practice and, in turn, generate theory from that practice. The chapter outlines how dialogue was kernel to the learning partnership and how it influenced many aspects of our learning. This included the clarification of ideas, the learning of others, the development of a sense of mutual respect and how it was an opportunity for healing and creativity among others. The introduction of technology to extend educational conversations is also explored here. We conclude with a discussion on how the boundaries between professional development and academic research were crossed and diminished by the members of the learning community. The reader is given an insight into how we authors created, developed and nurtured our own learning partnership using a self-study approach to action research.

## Chapter 2 Action Research as the Glue in Professional Learning Partnerships

Here we reflect on our current insights into that first learning community in terms of how developing new understandings with others can provide the 'glue' for helping a community to come together and stick together. Because this process was based on our firm belief in the power of action research, we explore our current understanding of the term 'action research'. We explain the connections that we perceive to exist between self-study action research and the organic growth of a learning community. We outline how, as we entered the postdoctoral phase of our lives, we authors decided to extend our learning community and develop new ones. The chapter draws to a close with a discussion on the role of the leaders or conveners of a learning community.

## Chapter 3 Learning Communities as Sites of Transformation

Our understanding of learning communities, where people come together to share their learning experiences, is explained in this chapter. We outline some of the characteristics of an effective learning community, such as cooperation, collaboration, equality and trust. We describe a learning community that we convened and outline the learning that occurred, for both participants and convener. We explain how participants developed new knowledge about their practice, which they were able to articulate as a theory of their practice. These positive outcomes are indicative of the transformative potential of learning communities. This chapter looks at traditional approaches in academic and practical settings and examines the theory–practice divide that is often evident in these settings. Theories of inclusion and democracy are explored because we believe that a shift towards more inclusive and democratic ways of working with schools and communities is a necessity for colleges and universities trying to fulfil their mission in the education of teachers (Zeichner 2010).

## Chapter 4 A Theoretical Explanation of the Practical Significance of Learning Communities

The theme of the traditional separation of theory and practice is continued in this chapter, and the reasons for the dichotomy are explored. We examine the various efforts to reconcile the theory–practice divide, in particular the role of critical pedagogy and self-study action research in this regard. We discuss the potential of learning communities to create hybrid spaces that could bridge the gap between academic and practitioner knowledge, and in the process move from an Aristotelian either/or to a Platonic both/and approach. Developing partnerships through participating in learning communities is explored and this process builds on the perspectives of Wenger's communities of practice (1998) and Sergiovanni's school communities (1994). The chapter describes how a learning community enables participants to make the transition from a collection of 'I's to a collective 'we' as they share ideas and resources in a collaborative environment. The examples of learning communities that we use in this chapter demonstrate how we created authentic, effective and sustainable partnerships through self-evaluation and self-study action research.

## Chapter 5 Professional Conversations as Integral to Self-Study Action Research for CPD

In this chapter, we look at how the provision of spaces for professional conversations can lead to reflective, self-evaluative and emancipatory practice. We examine what teachers can learn from talking with one another about their educational concerns, values and day-to-day teaching practice, and we present an argument for how, as Clark (2001) says, teacher talk can become a powerful medium for teacher learning and professional development. We look at what some participating teachers have to say about their involvement in our learning community and their learning within professional conversation spaces. We question if a Continuing Professional Development course can offer an authentic conversation space when presented in a solely online environment.

## Chapter 6 Initial Teacher Education and School–College Partnerships: The Potential Role of Self-Study Action Research

In this chapter we explore some of the complexities of the ITE school placement or practicum experience. We look at how we sought to foster a 'researcherly disposition' – particularly an 'action researcherly disposition' (Sullivan et al. 2016) amongst undergraduates in a small ITE college context, and how our process might be adapted to suit a school–college partnership. The responses of participating students are included as are some case studies. We examine what the potential learning might be for all the stakeholders – participating student teachers and education lecturers – as well as the potential significance that this approach could have for the school–college partnership.

## Chapter 7 Tapping into Experiential Knowledge in Whole-School Communities

Our focus, in this chapter, is on accessing and enhancing the experiential knowledge of the teacher and of whole schools by forming learning communities to conduct action research into their practice. Using stories from our projects, we offer ways to get teachers fully on board within whole-school learning communities. These descriptions are explained against theories of learning and motivation and our processes of generating theory from practice. This knowledge could be invaluable in school–college partnerships for initial teacher education and for mentoring teachers throughout their careers.

## Chapter 8 What's in This for Me? From the Perspective of Participating Teachers, Teacher Educators and Leaders

Finally we tell of key transformative moments which participants, from an array of learning communities, shared with us. We account for the importance of these events by relating them to the literatures on learning, psychology and epistemology. In the second part of the chapter, conveners of learning communities tell of their learning. This included critically examining the processes by which they supported a variety of groups. They cite the importance of open and non-coercive, differentiated and strength-based approaches. Conveners of learning communities rarely have opportunities to discuss their learning and to critically examine its significance and challenges. In this chapter you will hear what they have to say.

# What is new in this book

Many of the research projects included in the book are first-hand accounts, emanating from our own practice, and based on our experience of working as a learning community. Rather than reporting and analyzing learning partnerships in education from an external perspective, as is often the case in traditional educational research, this book contains the authentic voices of the practitioners as insider researchers. Drawing on our own experiences, we show how our learning journeys, in setting up learning communities and researching learning partnerships across the education spectrum, can benefit other teachers and teacher educators as they engage in similar initiatives. We demonstrate the potential of self-study action research as a form of professional learning in educational communities by using examples from our own learning partnerships.

This book will be helpful for teachers working within school–college partnerships, who seek to develop a critical and questioning disposition. It describes and explains how to engage in processes of enquiry within learning communities so that teachers have the potential to become influential in their own educational settings (Carr and Kemmis 1986; Kincheloe 2003; McNiff and Whitehead 2005; Schön 1995). Although we cannot engage in actual conversation here with you, our readers, the 'Reflective opportunity' sections in each chapter provide a framework to enable you to engage critically with the ideas presented. While the book contains guidelines and suggestions, it is neither prescriptive nor coercive: the whole tenor of the book is invitational. We are committed to the idea that teachers need to take ownership of their own learning process and that they have much to contribute to their own professional development. Therefore, we are not telling people what to do but are inviting them to walk an educational journey along with us. Our hope is that, through the process of critical reflection on their practice and through their endeavours to live to their values, they will experience the life-enhancing educational benefits for themselves and their students, as we have done over many years of engaging in self-study action research.

# 1

# A Professional Learning Partnership

*Máirín Glenn*

## Introduction

Some years ago, Bernie, Caitriona, Mary and I, Máirín, embarked on our journey of learning together. We met initially as individuals who were interested in engaging in self-study action research towards doctoral accreditation. What began as a chance meeting, gradually became a learning partnership with others and, as years went by, our collegiality blossomed into a firm friendship. Ours is a story of personal and professional learning that began within our own small community, but that extended and transformed itself into a wider and broader community over time. Here, in this chapter, I examine the initial stages of how our learning community came into being, having emerged from a thirst for learning. I explain how, intuitively, we established ourselves as a small learning community and how we, as practitioners, wished to explore self-study action research. We wished to extend our learning so as to enhance our practice and, in turn, generate theory from our practice. I describe how each member of the community brought their own professional identities to the learning community and how they helped shape and mould its structure. I describe how dialogue was at the heart of our partnership and how it influenced many aspects of our coming together such as the clarification of ideas, the learning of others, developing a sense of mutual respect and our own sense of well-being and creativity. I explain how I developed a web space and a chat room to extend our educational conversations and outline how we crossed the boundaries between professional development and academic research.

In this chapter I explore:

- our first learning community as it evolved from a group of different people, from various contexts and diverse interests coming together to learn
- the notion of professional identity in a learning community
- the role of dialogue within our learning community
- use of technology to extend our learning
- the interface between professional development and research.

## Different people: different contexts

Our beginnings as a learning community originated in humble surroundings. Our first meetings took place in a school hall and in a classroom in a secondary school. We came together as a diverse group of people with a shared interest in reflective practice and practitioner research. Somehow, from this common interest, we four authors, Bernie, Caitriona, Mary and myself, began a learning journey some seventeen years ago, which has grown to the extent that we have now established ourselves, along with others, as a fairly vibrant learning community (see www.eari.ie for example).

Over that period of time, we have forged a strong, warm and loving friendship, but in the beginning we were four individual people, strangers to one another, from different parts of the country, studying four disparate aspects of education. We initially came together because of our interest in action research, as our masters' programmes drew to a close. We had each, separately, heard that a group was being convened in Ireland which would establish itself as a research group that would, possibly, explore action research to PhD level. It would be an opportunity for us to engage in some robust action research as we clarified our values, reflected on our practice, engaged in critical reflection and sought to improve our practice or our understanding of it as we generated our educational theory from our own practice.

An initial meeting was held in a school and a large, vociferous group attended. As someone with little confidence in the field of action research, and as someone who knew no one at the meeting, I felt I lacked the social nous demanded by the action research conversations that flitted and whirled around the room – a feeling that is commonly felt by newcomers to learning communities (see Wenger-Trayner and Wenger-Trayner 2015) and where newcomers perceive themselves as incompetent as they engage in 'negotiating identity in a new setting' (Fenton-O'Creevy et al. 2015: 34). The evening drew to a close with an invitation to everyone who was interested to register. Bernie, Caitriona, Mary and I were among those who expressed our interest, not realizing the influence the evening would have on our lives from there onward.

As I recall this evening, I am reminded of the almost prophetic quality of Wenger's words:

> Being alive as human beings means ... we interact with each other and with the world and we tune our relations with each other and with the world accordingly. In other words we learn.
>
> Over time, this collective learning results in practices that reflect both the pursuit of our enterprises and the attendant social relations. These practices are thus the property of a kind of community created over time by the sustained pursuit of a shared enterprise. It makes sense, therefore to call these kinds of communities *communities of practice*. (Wenger 1998: 45)

We were quite unaware, at this time, of our future emergence as a 'community of practice'. By the time the study group was established, there was a core group of about fifteen people from diverse backgrounds, of which my co-authors and I were part. We found our academic home in the University of Limerick, Ireland. As we settled into our doctoral studies, the four of us, Bernie, Caitriona, Mary and I immersed ourselves into that larger core group. As the months of study rolled by, we began to see the power of communication and collaboration, of sharing and critiquing, indeed of participating in a learning community as a rich opportunity and stimulus for learning. Like Tannehill and MacPhail (2016: 4) we saw that as our community developed, we came 'to appreciate one another as thinkers and as learners'.

In the beginning, we were a group of people studying individually for PhDs, who met together for one or two weekends each semester to discuss our emergent understanding of the underpinning principles of self-study action research and living theory (Whitehead 1989). Each meeting gave us a new sense of energy and engagement. We began to get to know one another socially. We also found that our face-to-face sessions gave us an opportunity to engage in critical conversations and discuss issues that were of professional interest to us.

Our tutor had a particular way of working that somehow enhanced our fledgling community. She encouraged us to think for ourselves and to question any loose assumptions we might make, to discuss all areas of interest first in small groups and then as a whole group, and to engage in critical reflection. She rarely gave us the answers to any questions; instead she encouraged us to think, read, engage with ideas, problematize our ideas, discuss, critique, engage in dialogue and indeed, become a community of practice. Sometimes we were a little frustrated by our continuous search for unattainable truths, but mostly we grew and learned. We read and critiqued various academic writers and these conversations ignited our learning, sparked our imagination and energized us for further study.

## *We authors*

At this time, the four of us were part of the larger PhD research group that met for seminars in the University of Limerick. Even though we four were all primary school teachers, our backgrounds and research interests were not closely aligned. Caitriona was interested in exploring how she might live up to her values around working with her students who had specific learning difficulties (dyslexia) while Mary was exploring how she might develop dialogue and critical thinking processes with her primary school students. Bernie's interests lay in the area of social justice and how she might establish a more equitable and inclusive learning environment for her students from the travelling community. My own interests lay in developing a more holistic approach to teaching and learning that embedded technology as part of the process.

Our personalities differed as dramatically as our areas of interest: Bernie is practical, reflective, funny and logical and has a no-nonsense approach to life. She has a positive outlook on everything and if she chooses to do something, she rarely sees any obstructions between herself and her goal. She is an avid storyteller and has an amazing capacity to make connections between people from all parts of the world. Caitriona is extremely kind and has the ability to see a need or vulnerability where others might not. She is a highly organized person, who keeps everyone on track and has the ability to keep her eye on the 'bigger' picture when the rest of us might get swallowed up in minutiae. Mary is a voracious reader and a great talker. She is generous and warm, a dreamer, an imaginer, a person who likes to question assumptions and is very sociable. She is a good networker and has a wicked sense of humour and terrible sense of direction. I am the 'hippy chick' of the group and I am also the person who experiments with using technology to extend and enhance our dialogue. I try to hold the values we embrace in the forefront of my thinking, and I try to focus on what we are doing and the fundamental reasons for doing it. We are a diverse group of women, and yet, somehow, we were drawn to one another within that larger study group. As you read through the book, you will encounter the diverse tones of our voices even though we wrote and edited our book collaboratively.

As members of the larger study group, we all settled down to the serious work of doing a PhD, and wrestled with ideas around epistemology and knowledge creation. My own reflections at the time showed how I called the group a 'professional conversation group':

In recent times, as part of my doctoral research, I have found myself becoming involved in a professional conversation group with my colleagues in research. We meet on the university campus and have exciting, stimulating dialogue and knowledge-generating weekend-long sessions twice during every semester under the guidance of our tutor in a caring environment. I use the word 'caring' in a non-sentimental manner. Instead I refer to the notion of a safe environment, whereby doctoral researchers may dialogue with one another in an open attentive learning space, wherein every voice is listened to and dialogue may take place without fear of ridicule or offence. (Reflective Journal, April 2002)

We learned that knowledge was not necessarily found solely in textbooks. We saw it emerge in the conversations we had with colleagues, in our attempts to express our ideas and in our listening to others. We found our learning to be socially constructed. Like McDermott (1999: 16) we felt that

learning traditionally gets measured on the assumption that it is a possession of individuals that can be found inside their heads ... learning is not in heads, but in the relationships between people. Learning is in the conditions that bring people together and organize a point of contact that allows for particular pieces of information to take on a relevance; without the points of contact, without the system of relevancies, there is not learning, and there is little memory. Learning does not belong to individual persons, but to the various conversations of which they are a part.

My own reflective writing from that time continued:

Shulman (1999) suggests that for learning to occur, for development in our thinking to take place, we must become involved in a dual process whereby we must first articulate what we know, share it with others and then internalise the newly shaped knowledge ... I believe that our conversation group in the university draws on the knowledge described by this type of learning ... Our group is also critical in its reasoning and discussions. I feel very privileged to be a participant in my current learning environment. I am part of an exciting group, where our learning is stimulated as we speak and listen, where communication and dialogue is the scaffolding of our learning (Shulman ibid.). (Reflective Journal, June 2002)

We learned that we actually had the potential to generate our own knowledge and theory from our practice (see McDonagh et al. 2012; Sullivan et al. 2016). A key element of our action research process was to make a contribution to theory which was generated from within our practice. Our dialogue, as a community of learners, gave us an opportunity to ensure that our emergent theory was both robust and authentic. We found that Wenger's (1998) reminder of the importance of individuals' perspectives on learning, as well as their awareness of their epistemological stance, was at work in our group. We found that we were becoming both reflective and critical with regard to our 'own discourses for learning' (ibid.: 9) and we were beginning to 'participate inventively' (ibid.: 10) so that our community might prosper.

# Professional identity in our learning community

While many of the people in our PhD learning community were teachers, some were not. However, all were studying various aspects of education in its broadest sense. The notion of professional identity is inextricably tied up with the idea of learning partnership. Wenger-Trayner and Wenger-Trayner (2015) claim that 'our identities come to embody the landscape [of practice] through our experience of it. They become personalized reflections of the landscape, its practices and its boundaries.' (ibid.: 20). I think most of the participants in our PhD study group would agree that our learning partnership had a strong influence on our sense of identity (and our practice) as educators. However, many of us approached our group with decades of experience in our respective fields and we each had a strong and comfortable sense of our professional identity. That sense of identity helped to mould the landscape of our learning community. Sachs (2005: 15) says: 'Teacher professional identity ... stands at the core of the teaching profession. It provides a framework for teachers to construct their own idea of "how to be", "how to act" and "how to understand" their work and their place in society.' This idea of one's professional identity being at the heart of the profession, providing the framework to understand practice and to develop ontological and epistemological commitments, is not solely in the remit of the teacher. It appears to be true for other caring professions also. See, for example, Goldie (2012) and Wiles (2013), who write similarly about professional identity in the medical profession and for social workers. As practitioners, we seem to express our identity in the practice we undertake. For teachers, Palmer states it simply: 'Teaching holds a mirror to the soul ... we teach who we are' (n.d.: 1).

The following extract from my own reflective diary at the time demonstrates this:

> In order to live towards my values, I try to create learning situations and environments where my colleagues and my class may transcend the walls of the classroom, the barriers of distance and disadvantage, and

communicate in online learning areas. Freire's (1970: 65) notion of 'Without dialogue there is no communication and without communication there can be no true education' is kernel to my thinking around these issues. (Reflective Journal, April 2002)

I was beginning to learn that I was expressing my own self as I engaged in my everyday practice as a teacher – my practice was an articulation of my own identity and the values I held. Others in our group had similar experiences. For example, Bernie said:

> My experience of working with children from the Travelling Community to date has caused me to alter my view of Travellers as the Other, or as being on the fringes of society and to see them instead as an essential entity in Irish society, contributing to that society through the richness of a culture that can be traced back to the twelfth century. This new, enlightened, reconceptualised view of Travellers obliges me to present a rights-based model of education for these students, instead of a deficit model that posits them as a sub-group of the school population, in need of remediation. (Extract from group conversation, June 2002)

Bernie was exploring her emerging ideas around her work with travellers and found that not only was her teaching mirroring her soul, but that she was also beginning to change and reshape her thinking. Sachs says: 'Importantly, teacher identity is not something that is fixed nor is it imposed; rather it is negotiated through experience and the sense that is made of that experience' (2005: 15). We each came to our learning community with our individual sense of professional identity that was already established. Many of us found that our identity was then further moulded and negotiated by our own internal dialogues, as outlined above, and in the interactions and the new learning that emerged within our community. Each of these interactions involved dialogue, which is the foundation on which a learning community is based.

## Reflective opportunity

Bearing in mind that we 'teach who we are', take a moment to describe what you perceive as your professional identity. (This will probably evolve over time.)

Can you recognize any areas in your practice where you might see elements of your identity mirrored?

Are there possibly some elements of your identity that should be mirrored in your practice – or maybe some that should not?

# Dialogue and our community of learning

Our community of practice and learning emerged organically from our own passion for growth and learning. We found that dialogue and conversation lay at the heart of our learning and formed the mainstay of our learning community. Many writers like to differentiate between the terms 'conversation' and 'dialogue': 'Dialogue is not like other forms of communication (chatting, arguing, negotiating, and so on). Dialogue is an activity directed toward discovery and new understanding', according to Burbules (1993: 8). But Gadamer (1979) sees conversation as a way of coming to an understanding, where knowledge is not an external fixed entity awaiting discovery. He sees it as a process wherein participants have their own prejudices as they enter the conversation and they try to understand the 'horizon of understanding' (1979: 347) of the other. Like Brookfield and Preskill (2005), we perceive that both terms embrace critical engagement and lead towards clarity of thought and new learning, in terms of 'reciprocity and movement, exchange and inquiry, cooperation and collaboration, formality and informality' (ibid.: 6). In our learning community, we tried to embrace dialogue and dialogical ways of knowing, so that nobody was trying to be a winner so that there was 'no attempt to gain points or to make your particular view prevail' (Bohm 2004: 7). We found that dialogue was the single most important ingredient in our learning community.

As we learned, we found commonalities and areas of disagreement, shared interests and areas of disinterest as well as sprinklings of humour, laughter and conviviality. Sometimes the tone of our dialogue was formal and we used academic terms and language that were appropriate for our doctoral studies. At other times our tone was casual and lighter. While dialogue was kernel to all aspects of our learning process, we found that dialogue influenced some elements of our engagement most profoundly. I will discuss these elements in more detail below. They included *the clarification of ideas, personal learning, the learning of others, as a form of mutual respect, healing–well-being and creativity.*

## *Dialogue for clarification*

As we engaged in dialogue with one another, we found that by trying to articulate our thoughts, we prepared them in our minds for sharing with others. We seemed to gain clarity into the ideas we were aiming to communicate even though they may have been only partially formulated in our thoughts before we came to share them. This in-depth digging into our own beliefs helped us to tease out our ideas. We found, like Danielson (2016), that being asked to articulate our ideas and express them aloud, so that others would hear what we were thinking, helped us to clarify our thoughts for ourselves. On hearing ideas, whether fully formulated or not, some members of our group, like myself, liked to 'digest' ideas and preferred a slower, 'percolation' process of engaging with ideas. Writing to one another and sharing our ideas in a kind of 'slow motion' was helpful for us. For others, a 'quick-fire' round of questions and oral responses was what they needed to clarify their thinking. Both of these models of dialogue, as well as many others on the continuum between the 'quick-fire' and 'slow motion', featured in our engagements with one another. As we listened to the responses of those around us, we reshaped our own ideas in response to what we had heard and understood from others. Sometimes our ideas became more ingrained, and we held solidly to them. On other occasions, when engaging in dialogue, our ideas changed and grew. We found that our learning and growth often took place when we questioned our ideas and either held more firmly to them or modified them. Like Tannehill and MacPhail (2016), learning was a primary goal for us, but we also found value in the *process* of learning.

## *Dialogue for personal learning*

When we began working and studying for a PhD, many of us had not envisaged how dialogue and being in community with one another would hold such a key role for us. Our learning community developed without any strong sense of formality or awareness of rules. We were simply a group of people who wanted to research how we might improve our practice or improve our understanding of it. We, as action researchers, wanted to explore our values and examine how we might live them more fully in our professional lives. We sought to examine how we might learn in the context of our lived experiences (Wenger 1991). As we spoke with one another and articulated our understandings of the topic for discussion, we listened to one another and grappled with our shared, and often misunderstood, meanings. Burbules and Rice (1998: 409) suggest that 'once one embarks in a dialogical exchange, various degrees of convergent or divergent understandings might result … (a) agreement and consensus (b) not agreement but a common understanding (c) not a common understanding but an understanding of differences (d) little understanding but a respect across differences (e) irreconcilable and incommensurable difference'. In our group, we found that while we often experienced certain amounts of agreement, there were many occasions when there were irreconcilable differences but we utilized our understanding of difference and a respect across differences to move our thinking along. Arriving at a stage where there is 'incommensurable difference' in the shared understandings sought by those in a group may be uncomfortable or frustrating for many. However, learning, at quite a deep level, will probably have occurred for many: 'The role of the other ... in professional conversations is critical; they supply the mirror, the sounding board, the sympathetic (and indeed sometimes challenging voice)'. (Danielson 2016: 5). In one dialogue Mary said:

> In our discussion about influence Chris, Paula (not their real names) and I immediately positioned ourselves in the role of educators rather than learners. This is interesting, given that our discussions took place in the context of us as students. Initially we took what our tutor described as 'a pejorative view' of the word 'influence'. We spoke about issues of exerting influence and power. Exploring our understandings of the abuse of power in a classroom context led us to think around the issue of indoctrination ... It brings me now to the whole idea of whether I am indoctrinating or merely influencing others, in general, when I am teaching in my particular style and, in particular, when I am doing this research. (Extract from group conversation, January 2002)

Mary's reflections here clearly show how others in the group provided her with a 'sounding board' for developing her thinking and understanding.

## *Dialogue in the learning of others*

As our learning community developed and grew, we became aware that dialogue not only enhanced our own learning as we engaged in conversations with others, but it also enhanced the learning of others. This was the case even when our own knowledge was tentative and not fully understood by ourselves. Sometimes, as we shared our 'half-baked' thoughts, we were aware that they were not fully formulated as we communicated them. We acknowledged this to one another as we shared them, but, somehow, others learned from the discussion around these ideas. I subsequently developed an online space for writing and communicating. We called our site the *Site for Half-Baked Ideas* as an acknowledgement of the emergent nature of many of our ideas and I will discuss it later in this chapter. Gadamer sees conversation as a process where participants have their own prejudices as they enter the conversation and they try to comprehend the 'horizon of understanding' (1979: 347) of the other. We found that something magical happened in the course of the dialogue: somehow through the sharing of both strong beliefs, as well as our not-fully formed ideas with others, a nugget of insight was often illuminated, a new learning was inspired. As I wrote at that time:

> MacLure (1996) has some interesting thoughts about turning points in action research. She suggests that when events such as 'critical incidents'

or 'epiphanies' are narrated, the person has to be already predisposed towards this new change of thought, before the blinding flash of insight. The blinding flash may not be as serendipitous as we might first think, it may be a natural culmination of a period of preparation. (Extract from group conversation, May 2002)

In the course of people grappling with ideas, listening to others, articulating their understandings and questioning others, new insights were born. Being aware of the potential of your own influence on the thinking of others and perhaps the changing of lifelong beliefs of others reminds us of our responsibilities as we speak. Sometimes, a throwaway remark can have a devastatingly upsetting effect on someone just as easily as such a remark can also inspire someone to become a 'better' version of themselves. As participants in dialogue, we learned that we needed to be aware of the responsibility we hold as we try to use our words wisely and effectively.

## Dialogue as an expression of mutual respect

Following on from thinking about our responsibility to others as we engaged in dialogue, we found that we developed a sense of mutual respect towards one another. Frequently we spoke with passion and fervour about our ideas and about our work. Our voices might often be raised, our eyes lit with enthusiasm and our words might tumble out with speed and excitement. But, right alongside that passion, we quickly realized that we needed to speak with respect and a sense of awareness of the others involved in the dialogue. We often discussed Buber and his thinking on 'I–It' and 'I–Thou' relationships. We, nearly unconsciously, began to embrace his ideas as an unwritten code to frame how we engaged with one another. Buber says:

> To be aware of a man [sic], therefore, means in particular to perceive his [sic] wholeness as a person determined by the spirit; it means to perceive the dynamic center which stamps his every utterance, action, and attitude with the recognizable sign of uniqueness. (Cited in Yoshida 2002:134).

In our conversations in our online chat room, we had the following exchange around getting to grips with Foucault's ideas around capillary actions of power:

**Máirín:** About Foucault and capillary actions of power, I have not found the actual word but I did find this: Foucault (1980a) when talking about power within the French monarchy said it was 'rambling and full of loopholes … But the economic changes of the eighteenth century made it necessary to ensure the circulation of effects of power through progressively finer channels, gaining access to individuals themselves, to their bodies, their gestures and all their daily actions.' This is from page 151 in 'The Eye of Power' in 'Power/Knowledge' edited by Colin Gordon. This sounds like capillaries to me. On page 255 of the same book Gordon himself uses the term 'capillary' ...

**Geraldine:** Well done Máirín, that sounds like it alright. I love how complex and slippery Foucault is, don't you? (Extract from chat room, November 2002)

In this extract from our conversations, Geraldine's response is respectful and empathetic as I try to learn more about Foucault. Both of us are participating in dialogue in a mutually respectful manner as we grapple with new concepts. Similarly, Bohm et al. (1991) outline the importance of mutual respect in dialogue: 'A Dialogue is essentially a conversation between equals' (Bohm et al. 1991). As our community grew and established itself, we found that mutual respect for one another soon became a hallmark of our engagement with one another.

## *Dialogue for healing and well-being*

Because we were studying our own practice, we were all working full time as well studying for our doctorates. While most of us felt that this was a fruitful and productive time of our lives, it also brought its own set of challenges in terms of pressure on our professional, personal and home lives. Sometimes, if we were struggling professionally, academically or even personally, our dialogue gave us an opportunity to share our concerns with colleagues. Often, the sharing of our concerns helped to ease our stress and even soothe our pain. We may not have found a solution to our problems or an antidote to any hurt we may have experienced, but we found solace in the process of sharing our struggles with others who listened with compassion.

Recently, I heard Ernie Stringer and Jack Whitehead, both leading scholars in the field of action research, debate inconclusively about whether it was from a place of pain or from a place of joy that people came together to enter into dialogue around practice with one another and engage in action research. Our own experience was that we came together for educational discussions both from places of joy and pain, as well as from a desire for adventure and stepping into the unknown. Thich Nhat Hanh reminds us: 'We have to believe that by engaging in dialogue with another person, we have the possibility of making a change within ourselves, that we can become deeper' (Hanh 1995: 9). We did become 'deeper' as we engaged in dialogue, and very often we were nurtured, inspired and healed by the process.

## *Dialogue for creativity*

In our learning community, many of our more formal discussions were on a specific topic. We discussed issues such as hegemony, educative influence, power, knowledge and the meaning of education, for example. Frequently however, as we broke into to our discussion groups, the discussion flowed not only in many expected directions but also in unpredictable ones. New thinking and new ideas often emerged as we spoke and listened to one another. Very often these unpredictable outcomes gave rise to new creativity or new ideas which sometimes influenced our professional practice. Deverell and Moore (2014) suggest that links and connections between dialogue and creative and innovative practice are very strong and that institutions should formally create opportunities for learning communities to nurture such dialogue.

We experienced what Bohm describes as a 'stream of meaning' (Bohm 1996: 7). Bohm saw dialogue as a 'stream of meaning flowing among and through us and between us'. I will discuss Bohm's idea of the stream of meaning in greater detail in the next chapter. Bohm saw the flow of meaning reaching the whole group, from which 'new, creative understandings may emerge ... something new, which may not have been in the starting point at all' (ibid.). We found that our dialogue flowed in many different directions, many of which were inspiring and thought-provoking, and the outcomes of our discussions were unforeseeable.

# Reflective opportunity

You have seen how we used dialogue to not only enhance our learning but to extend our learning process too. How might you use dialogue to enrich your learning?

Take a moment now to reflect on and describe some instances of different types of dialogue which you have experienced.

# Using technology to extend our dialogue

As our learning community carried on, we quickly developed a sense that our face-to-face sessions were not long enough or frequent enough to have in-depth discussions and to continue our excavation of ideas as deeply as we might have liked. The members of our group lived at a distance from one another and in an effort to diminish that sense of distance and to continue our conversations, we established an email group initially, where everyone was able to be in contact with one another as a group. It has to be remembered that at that time, not everyone had easy access to email, and so, while we emailed our ideas and thinking to one another and responded to one another, we used traditional postal mail as well so as to include everyone in the group.

The following is a sample of the email correspondence from our group at that time:

> In our tutor's last letter she mentioned 'multiple epistemologies' and I fear the phrase has me slightly perplexed. Can anyone explain it to me please? Is it referring to multiple ways of knowing ... is this connected to multiple intelligences?
>
> Reply via email from M. 01-04-2002:
>
> It makes sense to see it as multiple theories of knowing or multiple knowledge bases ... I am not sure though how they are tied in with Gardner per se ... ok theories of knowing could be 'ways of knowing', I suppose, so perhaps we all understand the theories in different ways? Or we all interpret/apply the theories in ways that make sense to us ... could that be it?
>
> And another reply via email from C. 07-02-2002:
>
> Multiple intelligences did not strike me as a synonym for multiple epistemologies at first. Epistemology, I think, means a way of viewing knowledge. For example, knowledge can be viewed as a box full of wisdom to be passed on, or as growing in wisdom by sharing/dialoguing with others, or as something which changes as we grow in it. All of these views (epistemological stances) can inform our choice of methodology ... But I think the multiple intelligences theory is about knowledge from different perspectives. (From Glenn 2006: 243)

We can see from this excerpt that we used email to clarify and discuss ideas that were new to us. While none of us perceived ourselves as 'knowers' or as having the answers, together we tried to share our own understanding so that collectively we could grasp the meaning of the new ideas more comprehensively.

While group email was helpful, initially, in assisting us to tease out concepts we found difficult, in clarifying our thinking and in helping us to articulate and modify our thinking, we found that after a time, the system needed refining. We found that email was too 'clunky' and unwieldy to use when our responses to one another become more complex. It has to be remembered that there were no online, shared learning/discussion spaces or Virtual Learning Environments such as Blackboard or Moodle, for example, available to us then. My reflective journal from that time stated:

I have learned through conversations in the university that our meetings are inspiring and highly thought-provoking, and my greatest learning takes place in the days and weeks after the event. My mind buzzes with thoughts and reflections on our discussions. But I have left my safe haven of the university and my colleagues in research have returned to their own workplaces and their words of wisdom are difficult to recall. The difficulty of meeting only twice every semester is that many outreach doctoral research colleagues do not have the opportunity to dialogue except at these meetings in the university. (Reflective Journal, April 2002)

I then decided to establish an online space for publishing our most current ideas for ourselves as a group, privately. I called it *Site for Half-Baked Ideas* (as described earlier) and it comprised of a platform for publishing our writing as well as a providing a private chat room. The more formal *Space for Half-Baked Ideas* site was a private online space for our group, where people posted their most current pieces of draft writing, reflections and ideas. We responded to one another and published our responses also. (You have seen extracts from this online space above.) It worked a little like a blog would today, but at the time, people in our group emailed their writing to me and I published it on our group web space. Our chat room worked a little differently in that inputs were much shorter and the language was more informal and everyone was able to input their own text.

More modern-day proponents of 'situation connectedness' such as Whitaker et al. (2015) suggest that educators grow and learn not only by opening Twitter accounts and participating in Professional Learning Networks (PLNs) but also through engaging in conversations by email, phone calls, handwritten notes and face-to-face. We used all of these elements in our initial learning community, (except Twitter because it had not been founded at that time).

The language we used in our chat room was more casual than the formal contributions to The *Space for Half-Baked Ideas*:

**Mary:** I'd be curious, Máirín, to see what people in our group think about our teaching obligations ... good idea for a discussion!

**Máirín:** I wonder if we're all tweaking within our systems. You remember D talked about Huberman and 'professional tinkering' within the curriculum ... remember his ideas about the oval circuit being the curriculum and maybe the best we can do is professionally tinker with what's there?

**Mary:** Good point Máirín. I think we are very fortunate to be in such a relatively free situation too! Tinkering with the curriculum would have you fired in some jurisdictions.

**Máirín:** Maybe if people didn't do some professional tinkering we'd never move on in our thinking. How about this Mary? I'm reading Holt at the moment and he talks about walls in education and says if we don't push the walls out they will push us in. If we do not try to improve our life space with more freedom of choice and action then we will surely end up with less. I believe that this is what is happening with the new curriculum as well. We're given huge freedom but we don't use it. We're looking for the textbooks and the work books and so on. (Glenn 2006: 246)

As I reflect now on the online spaces I created for our community, I can see that they did extend the opportunities for enhancing our learning. They gave us an opportunity to talk to one another between our face-to-face meetings, to continue conversations that had begun as face-to-face engagements and to begin topics for dialogue that could be picked up at the next group meeting. They also gave us an opportunity to write using academic language, which for many of us was initially a challenge. While participating in our *Space for Half-Baked Ideas* site was unsatisfactory for some members of the group who had little or no internet access at the time or who were uncomfortable using it, I believe that, in general, it did help to extend and deepen our dialogue and enhance our learning.

## Learning community: is it for professional development or for research?

We found in our learning community that our engagement with one another, as we sought to extend our learning, softened the boundary between what many people might label 'Continuing Professional Development' (CPD) and what others called 'research'. Many outsiders who were not involved in our group found it difficult to understand the hybrid nature of our work. We felt that we were clearly doing research on our own practice, which informed how we might improve our practice, with the aim of generating theory from our learning in that process. We experienced both professional development and research merging into one.

CPD is broadly understood as the ongoing maintenance, improvement and development of the knowledge, skills and personal qualities required in professional life, after basic qualification. It may be gained both formally and informally and is expected to enhance practice. In some instances it is compulsory and in others it is voluntary. CPD is defined by Day as 'all natural learning experiences and those conscious and planned activities which are intended to be of direct or indirect benefit to the individual, group or school and contribute to the quality of education in the classroom' (Day 1999: 4).

Some of our engagement within our learning community drew from elements of CPD in that we discussed our professional practice and sought to improve and transform it. We developed a better knowledge of the skills we needed in our own teaching and learning as educators as well as gaining insight into why we engaged in the practices we did. We also had chosen to study our practice ourselves; it was neither a compulsory nor a required element of our professional development.

However, our form of research was key to our engagement with one another in our learning community. Bassey (1999: 35) defined research as 'systematic, critical and self-critical enquiry which aims to contribute to the advancement of knowledge'. As we have seen above, our communications with one another held being critical and self-critical as key elements to the process as we aimed to develop a deeper understanding of our practice. We used an action research approach for examining, through reflection and action, the wider educational context. We saw self-study action research as a 'deeply values-based approach to critical reflection on one's own work' as we collaborated with our colleagues in our learning community, with a view to becoming a better practitioner (Sullivan et al. 2016: 28). We adopted an 'action researcherly disposition' (ibid.: 69) in that we sought to critically reflect on our practice and aimed to live to our values. (We have drawn the term 'action researcherly disposition' (Sullivan et al. 2016) from Lingard and Renshaw's idea (2010) that all education practitioners and policymakers should adopt a 'researcherly disposition'). We made a claim to knowledge, theorized our work, presented evidence to demonstrate the validity of our claims and showed the significance of our research. Our subsequent PhD theses were accredited by the university and could therefore be clearly understood as quality research that attained the highest standard recognized by a university (see McDonagh 2007; Roche 2007; Sullivan 2006, for example).

The literatures of both self-study action research and communities of practice perceive their participants as boundary crossers (see Brydon-Miller et al. 2003; MacLure 1996; Wenger 1998; Wenger-Trayner and Wenger-Trayner 2015, for example). This intermingling of professional development with robust and validated research for accreditation was a cornerstone of our learning community. Our own professional development as educators was the basis for our research and our research in turn contributed not only to our own practice but also to the knowledge base for all those involved in education.

## To conclude

In this chapter, we examined how our first learning community comprised of different people, from different contexts, who had diverse research interests.

We also explored the notion of professional identity in our learning community and looked at the role of dialogue therein. For our community, the inclusion of technology extended and enhanced our learning from our face-to-face meetings. The interplay between the notion of professional development and undertaking action research is interesting and we explain how, for us, the boundaries between them were blurred.

Looking at our learning community retrospectively, I can now see how intuitively the community created itself. It seemed to emerge from a simple desire to engage in learning. This was not mandated by any university requirements. It came from an overwhelming desire to share ideas, difficulties and challenges and see learning as a social action. I can now see that the dialogue and communication in our learning community was nuanced by our group's innate attraction to self-study action research and living theory. We sought to articulate our values and improve our practice or our understanding of it. We engaged in critical reflection and searching dialogue. We critiqued our own ideas and those of other members of the group. Working with one another in a dialogical and collaborative manner leads 'not only to community and organizational change, but also to personal changes in the action researcher' (Brydon-Miller et al. 2003: 14). We had developed a passion for engaging in self-study for our learning partnership and for enhancing our practice. We had found, from our innate desire to learn as a community, that we could not only enhance our own learning but that of others also. We had found that this was a valuable and sustainable model of professional learning. Our personal changes were to bring about the next phase of our research and our development as a community of practice as we sought to share our insights with others. New learning communities were on the way!

# 2

# Action Research as the Glue in Professional Learning Partnerships

## *Máirín Glenn*

## Introduction

As we moved from our first community of practice and into the postdoctoral phase of our lives, we authors decided to extend our learning community. In the later sections of this chapter I relate how we did this. But first, let me outline our current insights into that first learning community, as in Chapter 1, in terms of how developing new understandings with others can provide the 'glue' for helping a community to come together and stick together. Because all of our work was underpinned by our firm belief in the power of action research, I dedicate a section of this chapter to examining our current understanding of the term 'action research'. I develop this idea by explaining the connections that we perceive exist between self-study action research and the organic growth of a community of practice. I then outline our own attempts to establish and develop new learning communities. The chapter draws to a close with a discussion on the role of the leaders or conveners of a learning community.

In this chapter I explore:

- the idea that shared meaning helps to keep learning communities vibrant and cohesive

- Our understanding of action research

- the links between action research and learning communities
- how we progressed to developing new learning communities.

## Shared meaning as the glue of learning communities

When we four authors reflect on our own 'mini-community', we are often struck by the differences in our own personalities, attitudes and beliefs. Yet, we continue to meet, to work together, to support one another and to find ways of expanding our learning. When we reflect on our continuing desire to work together we always come to the conclusion that our shared common ground is our passion for action research. We know what we mean when we discuss our efforts to improve our own practice, our engagement in critical thinking, our constant excavations to unearth our values, and our wish to share this passion with other educators. We have a shared understanding of how we see theory being generated from practice and how we value ourselves as knowledge creators. Reflecting now on our first community of practice, as outlined in Chapter 1, I remind you of Bohm's suggestion (2004: 7) that if, what he calls the spirit of dialogue is present in people, then the stream of meaning flows 'among and through us and between us' to the whole group. We believe that we have developed that shared meaning in the spirit of dialogue that flows through us and between us. Bohm claims that if there is a flow of meaning in the whole group, a new understanding may emerge. He describes this new meaning as being creative, and explains this new shared meaning as 'the "glue" or "cement" that holds people and societies together' (ibid.). We saw how new shared meanings and understandings flowed through our larger study group in Chapter 1 and helped to cement our relationships within that group. We found, as we began the postdoctoral phase of our lives, that it inspired us to develop new connections with others and establish new communities.

The Irish poet and philosopher John O'Donohue frequently reflected on community. Although O'Donohue did not write specifically about learning communities, his thoughts on communities of people transfer well to communities of learning. He laments the diminishing connections between increasingly busy human beings who inhabit our world as 'one of the deepest poverties in our times' (O'Donohue 2003: 133). He understands community as 'an ideal where the full identities of awakened and realized individuals challenge and complement one another' (ibid.). It is interesting to note that O'Donohue sees community as an ideal situation and includes challenges as an inherent part of his understanding of community. As members of a community, and as conveners of communities, we appreciate how challenges often strengthen the cohesion of the community. Like Csikszentmihalyi (2002), we believe that we can be strengthened by those who challenge our ideas. O'Donohue talks about the 'web of betweenness' which exists as 'the secret oxygen with which we secretly sustain each other' (ibid.: 133) and perceives that individual lives are deeply woven into the lives of others. We authors similarly seek to develop that 'web of betweenness' in the communities of practice in which we participate. We are aware of the fragility of the connections within our communities and we strive to nourish them. O'Donohue reminds us that as members of a community we have a responsibility to sustain our community: 'As in the rainforest, a dazzling diversity of life-forms complement and sustain each other; there is a secret oxygen with which we unknowingly sustain one another. True community is not produced, it is invoked and awakened' (O'Donohue 2003: 133). As members of a community of practice, we need to be aware of that responsibility we have to one another and of the secret oxygen that we can produce to help sustain one another.

For us four authors, it became apparent quite quickly that our 'shared meaning' had a direct link with our capacity for, and our interest in, adopting an action researcherly disposition to our work (Sullivan et al. 2016) – and, indeed, to our lives. We suggest that we, along with fellow education practitioners, might aim to improve our practice, critically reflect on and question our practice, and seek to live to our values as an innate and ongoing aspect of our approach to, and understanding of, education. We call this process an action researcherly disposition. We believe that adopting an action researcherly disposition is quite similar to Cochran-Smith and Lytle's idea of 'inquiry as stance' (Cochran-Smith and Lytle 2009a: 44). They state that inquiry as stance is not just an academic project or an intervention, but is a 'world view and a habit of mind – a way of knowing and being in the world of educational practice' (Cochran-Smith and Lytle 2009b: viii). They see it as a way of being, thinking and performing for those involved in education. It is part of a 'larger epistemological stance, or a way of knowing about teaching, learning and schooling, that is neither topic- nor project-dependent' (Cochran-Smith and Lytle 2009a: 44). Putting it simply, like Cochran-Smith and Lytle, we see self-study action research not just as an approach to research or an experimental intervention at work, we see it as a way of life, an attitude or disposition, both an ontology and an epistemology. We see it as something that becomes part of who we are and becomes almost as natural as breathing.

As we share our ideas with others in the various communities in which we participate or that we convene, we know that shared meaning and understanding are key to the sustainability of that community. We reach that shared meaning through dialogue, as outlined in Chapter 1. Shared meaning becomes the glue that holds a community of practice together, not through consensus or groupthink, but through mutual respect for difference of opinion and the quest for understanding. The process of sharing meaning outweighs and diminishes any sense of small-mindedness or desire to be the best that might arise.

# Reflective opportunity

Pause for a moment and think about how you might develop a researcherly disposition for yourself. What steps would you need to take, do you think?

Think about your place of work now. How might you establish or improve opportunities there to engage in dialogue around your practice?

# What do we mean by action research?

We are using the term 'action research' in an all-embracing manner here. As far as the four of us are concerned, we generally are referring to an approach to research that is an inherent part of our everyday lives as outlined above and is undertaken in our own place of work. It involves an exploration of our own practice, drawing on our values, with a view to improving that practice and generating theory from our learning in that process. The research is done *along* with participants, not *on* them.

We see action research as participatory and collaborative, as well as reflective and critical. We use the terms 'action research', 'self-study action research' and 'living theory' almost interchangeably. Action research is a practitioner-led approach to improving practice that draws on the researchers' own values as they attempt to improve their practice and live out their values in their practice (Whitehead 2015). As educational action researchers, we reflect critically on our practice and look to our students and colleagues to gain insight into our work. We read widely and critically and question any assumptions we may have made about our work (Brookfield 1995). We also plan and take some form of action to gain insight into our practice or to improve it and we use our values as lenses to evaluate the quality of our research. We invite critical friends to critique and evaluate our fledgling ideas as our research unfolds so as to make certain we are making sense and to ensure that our ideas are strong and robust. Action research, as we understand it, is very rigorous: evidence must be provided to support all claims and each claim must be held up to the lenses of the values held by the researcher to establish its validity. As the research process develops, action researchers establish a validation group to question and to verify the rigour and honesty of their findings. When we have produced validated evidence to support our claim, we can then declare that we have generated a theory of knowledge that has stemmed from the values we hold (see McDonagh et al. 2012; Sullivan et al. 2016; Whitehead and McNiff 2006).

While we are aware that many different interpretations of action research are held throughout the world (see the work of the following: Carr and Kemmis 1986; Collier 1945; Corey 1953; Elliott 2000; Lewin 1946, McNiff 1993; Stenhouse 1975 and Whitehead 1989, for example), we are welcoming of their input and learn from their interpretations as we journey towards our own better understanding of action research. Like Noffke (2009: 20) we 'look for ways to create convergences' in action research and like Brydon-Miller et al. (2003: 11) we acknowledge the disparate traditions of action research, and embrace the notion of knowledge as socially constructed and recognize that 'all research is embedded in a system of values' (ibid.).

## Reflective opportunity

If you feel, as you read this book, that you can contribute to our current understanding of action research, please make a note of your ideas and contact us via our website at http://www.eari.ie.

## Making the links between action research and communities of practice

We authors have found that studying and approaching our work in an action researcherly manner is empowering and energizing. As practitioners at the 'chalkface', we have been inspired not only by the insights we gained into our own practice but also by the insights we have gained from others studying their practice in an action researcherly manner. We have also felt energized by how we have been able to take charge of our own teaching and learning because we designed and took charge of making the changes we deemed to be necessary (see examples in Glenn 2006; McDonagh 2007; Roche 2007 and Sullivan 2006, for example). We link our sense of empowerment to the sense of autonomy that emerged for us as we took 'charge of critical features of the teaching and learning process in [our] setting' as outlined by Tannehill and MacPhail (2016: 3). This sense of empowerment and being at the helm of your own practice is key to how teachers continue to be motivated in their everyday practice. Morgan et al. (2010) have shown how the absence of positive events in a teacher's day-to-day practice impinge negatively on efficacy and motivation. Conversely, we have found that taking charge of your own practice, investigating it thoroughly and taking action toward improvement can generate a sense of motivation and positivity that is highly empowering.

Because self-study action research is always undertaken alongside others and is dependent on the input, insights and ideas of others, we can see the clear links between our participation in action research and partaking in a community of practice. Cochran-Smith and Lytle (2009a) also see the clear connections between teachers researching their practice and participating in a community: 'Taking an inquiry as stance means teacher and student teachers working within a community to generate local knowledge, envision and theorize their practice, and interpret and interrogate the theory and research of others' (ibid.: 44). As action researchers, we research our practice along with others rather than doing research on others and so a sense of community is established in the opening stages of an action research cycle. We also need *critical friends* as part of our action research. These are people with whom we discuss our new ideas and who offer us critical, robust, honest and supportive feedback. They may be colleagues, partners, fellow-researchers or others whose opinions we trust. They are kernel to the action research process and part of our community of practice as action researchers.

Our own initial community of practice was basically a community of learners who wanted to develop their own understanding of, and gain new insights into their practice using a self-study action research process, as outlined in Chapter 1. We found that our learning community established itself with ease. We knew that this was due, in part, to the fact that we were afforded great freedom of thought and encouraged to explore new ideas collectively by our tutor. We embraced the qualities of open-mindedness, responsibility and wholeheartedness that Dewey (1933) suggested as being key ways of reflective thinking. However, we embraced many of the elements of a learning community very solidly and very easily. Baker and Beames (2016) say that key elements of a successful community of practice include the following elements (among others):

> An on-going forum to discuss learning and teaching issues ... [the] early establishment of ownership of the CoP by the members; [the] informal nature of the meetings; [the] creation of a 'safe environment' in which to share ideas ... No designated leadership positions, though significant leadership ... a core of 'regulars' who are active in presenting and/or leading discussions. (Baker and Beames 2016: 77)

We felt very safe in our community of practice and there were no managers or leaders: just a group of regular participators. We clearly saw how our engagement in dialogue became core to how we progressed our learning not only as action researchers but also as members of a community of learning. Like Bohm et al. (1991), we experienced how the essence of dialogue 'is learning … as part of an unfolding process of creative participation between peers' (ibid.: 45). However, as we reflect now on our group and our thinking at that time, we can see that the establishment of our community was enhanced by the action research processes we were ourselves exploring at that time. When we think about how organically and intuitively our community of practice grew, it is evident that there are some clear commonalities between the community of learners that emerged spontaneously and the underlying principles of self-study action research. We can now see how the action research process and the growth of our community of learning seemed to enrich and supplement one another. In addition to dialogue, there were many other common areas. In particular, we see *reflection, critical engagement, epistemological inventiveness, collegiality,* participating in *grassroots*, bottom-up processes and *boundary crossing* as elements that are common to both a learning community and the action research process. I will now deal with each of these aspects.

## *Reflection as an element of a learning community and of action research*

As part of our ongoing studies of action research, we engaged in reflection-in action and reflection-on action (Schön 1983), which were key components of reflective practice and our approach to self-study action research (Sullivan et al. 2016). We kept reflective journals where we recorded events of the day and our reflections on them. We revisited our journal entries to re-examine our ideas and reflect critically on them and add to them or reshape them. This reflexivity is a core principle of action research and we embraced the ideas of Winter and Munn-Giddings (2001) as we saw how 'we need to be ready to see our own current interpretations of events (and our role in them) as data-to-be-analysed' (ibid.: 61). Revisiting journal entries and thinking and reflecting on them anew is a very important aspect of the action research process.

Similarly, in our dialogue and as part of our community of practice, we found that reflection on what we had said ourselves and on what had been said by others inspired us to meta-reflect (to reflect on our reflections) and to plan further dialogue. Many of us wrote in our reflective journals about our thoughts as we engaged in our own internal dialogue as a process of 'making sense, with others, of different forms of knowledge' (Fenton-O'Creevy et al. 2015: 59). You can examine our current work at www.eari.ie. We reflected as diligently on our dialogue with one another as on our journal entries on our work practices – you have seen examples of the quality of our dialogue in Chapter 1.

## Critical engagement as an element of a learning community and of action research

In our conversations in our learning community, we frequently sought to unpick and deconstruct the assumptions that we made in our everyday lives. Initially we found it difficult to see the hegemony that surrounds many of the 'givens' of everyday teaching and learning. We found it difficult to call 'the foundations and imperatives of the system itself into question' as outlined by Brookfield (2009: 297). The awakening of our ability to question assumptions was formed in the dialogue we had in our learning community. We gradually learned to question the power relationships that allow or promote one particular set of practices over another and to question whose interests are best served by this (Brookfield 2009), as the quality of our dialogue in our learning community deepened. For example, in our online discussion in May 2003, Caitriona showed her ability to question dominant assumptions in her class of students with specific learning difficulties: 'In creating opportunities for the voice of pupils to be heard, my research makes a space from which the voices of those not normally heard in education can be heard'. Bernie similarly questions hegemonic assumptions for her students: 'As much of the learning of children takes place in institutional settings, this bestows an onus on their educators to ensure high-quality educational opportunities that will result in effective learning for children. I am concerned that these opportunities may not be available to all children in equal measure.'

As action researchers, we utilize Brookfield's ideas around using four lenses to enhance our research process and to critically reflect on our practice. We tried to uncover our taken-for-granted assumptions as we viewed ourselves and our work through our own autobiographical lenses and personal reflections, through the lenses of our students and their insights and views, through the lenses of literature and current writings on our areas of interest and through the lenses of colleagues and their interpretations of how they perceived our engagement with our practice was progressing (Brookfield 1995). Using Brookfield's lenses enhanced our critically reflective processes and, at the same time, provided us with robust data to support our claims to knowledge as our research progressed.

## Epistemological inventiveness as an element of a learning community and of action research

As we familiarized ourselves with the processes of self-study action research and living theory, we examined ideas around epistemology. We asked questions like 'Who is a knower?', 'What counts as knowledge?' and 'Who decides?'

The posing of these questions was kernel to developing our understanding of our practice and our research. However, these musings were also part of how our learning community understood itself. We, like Wenger (1998), saw that we were generating our knowledge through our dialogue and that knowledge was not necessarily external to ourselves. We saw knowledge as socially constructed. We perceived that knowledge was generated by people, in a constructivist and relational manner, as outlined by Lowenthal and Muth (2008). Our learning community was pushing the boundaries of what was considered to be a conventional learning community in that factual knowledge was rarely 'given' to us. Much of our learning evolved from the questions posed and the understandings generated in the conversations in the group, along with drafting and redrafting writing processes.

## *Collegiality as an element of a learning community and of action research*

It is generally accepted that learning communities work in a collegiate and supportive manner (see, for example, Krovetz 1993; Owen 2014; Stoll et al. 2006). We found that in our learning community that we were: supportive of one another, encouraging, safe in our explorations of new ideas, respectful of one another, affirming, trusting, questioning and critical. One of our members commented, 'What we have here is a group of imaginative people with skills they are willing to share and open up their lives for scrutiny by their peers' (Extract from group conversation April 2002). This seems to draw on Barth's (1990) description of the key features of a learning community as being 'a place where students and adults alike are engaged as active learners in matters of special importance to them and where everyone is thereby encouraging everyone else's learning' (9). Interestingly, Wakefield (2001) suggests that a learning community that is too compliant and too agreeable is counterproductive. He believes that discomfort, in terms of disagreement, should be an element of a good learning community too, while Owen (2014) maintains that a good community of practice should be characterized by robust debate. Our learning community was characterized by collegiality through robust debate and critical dialogue. For example, in a conversation around whether educative influence was, in fact, a form of indoctrination, Mary made the point:

Because ... views can be debated and argued from different perspectives, putting only one view forward might reasonably be construed as indoctrination. Much of what we say in our classrooms is laden with our values. However, I would argue that while we can present children initially with our values, we must also give them the skills necessary for debating, questioning and challenging all such assumptions and helping them to either accept and make their own of these values or, after reasoned thought, to reject them. (Extract from online discussion, February 2002)

Action research embraces debate and dialogue, as researchers need to come together in a collegiate but critical manner to discuss new ideas and to engage in robust dialogue with critical friends. McNiff (2013) reminds us that while action research is an approach to examining one's own practice, it also becomes 'an enquiry ... with others acting as co-researchers and critical learning partners' (23). Being collegiate and supportive is key to action research as is the process of disrupting accepted assumptions and uncritical thinking, and engaging in critical dialogue.

## Grassroots movement as an element of a learning community and of action research

Our learning community, as PhD candidates, established itself organically, gradually and without a directive from PhD supervisors or university leaders. It emerged from within us gradually and instinctively. As members of that community, we had one overpowering aim and that was to learn. The impetus for instigating and developing as a learning community came from our own desires to learn and from our need to extend our learning so as improve our practice as educators. Interestingly, Baker and Beames (2016) suggest that the organic nature of how a learning community establishes itself is key to the success of that learning community.

Similarly, we found that in engaging in the action research process, and in seeking to improve our practice in our workplace, we were developing a 'bottom-up' approach to our professional learning. We were taking charge of our own learning in our places of work and drawing on our educational values to improve our work practices or our understanding of them. McNiff (2013) is convinced that action research is about the voice of the people in the streets and workplaces. Again, we were not following a directive from our Department of Education and Skills, we were merely following our own innate desire to improve our practice.

## Boundary crossing as an element of a learning community and of action research

As we engaged with one another in our learning community, we crossed many boundaries. While we were all involved in education, we were working in different levels of the system and in various aspects of it. We approached our work from different epistemological stances and embraced different understandings of the meaning of education, because as Wenger-Trayner and Wenger-Trayner (2015) rightly point out, as a group of people we lacked a shared history. However, boundaries can be places of unexpected learning. As a group we learned to listen to one another and gain new insights. We learned to hold our beliefs but to wear them lightly as we absorbed the views of others, discussed with them their justification for their beliefs, learned to understand their views and sometimes we had to readjust our own ideas subsequently. In action research processes, boundary crossing was at the heart of our work. We were learning to be researchers and practitioners, teachers and theorists: people who crossed the theory–practice divide every day. We were drawing on theory to support our thinking and improve our practice while, at the same time, we were aiming to generate theory from our practice. Through crossing real and imagined boundaries, we were generating new understandings and insights and transforming ourselves and our thinking and learning in the process.

It is interesting to note that some learning communities and groups of action researchers like to use rubrics to ensure that all the steps perceived to be necessary are taken (see DuFour 2011). We feel that our own community of learners was not very rubric-compatible. Our community developed more organically and naturally, from our own intellectual needs and desires. We had no specified target, goals or landmarks except to enhance our learning. For us, action research was far from being a box to be ticked; instead it formed the heartbeat of our learning community.

# Reflective opportunity

Take a moment now to outline areas in your own experience where you see commonalities between action research and participating in a learning community.

# Establishing new communities of practice

As our doctoral studies drew to a close, we experienced the sense of exhaustion that one feels at the end of a period of intensive study, as well as a sense of relief and a need for rest. But after that period of recovery was over, the sense of relief was replaced by a strange sense of emptiness. We found that we actually missed being action researchers. We missed the opportunity to engage in dialogue, think critically, interrogate our assumptions, reflect professionally and share practice. We missed the opportunity to have professional conversations with others and that delicious sense of exploring the unknown through dialogue. We realized we had now developed a yearning to reawaken our intellectual imaginations and share our understandings of the significance of action research and living theory (Whitehead 1989) with one another. We also wanted to share the magic of action research with others. Somehow, intuitively, and without making any great master plan, we authors began to construct a new learning community not only for ourselves but for others also.

Over the next few years, we subsequently established the following programmes and communities of practice: we convened professional learning groups and engaged in our own action research on that process (see Teaching Council of Ireland 2012a), we developed an online continuous professional development programme (CPD), we wrote books, we created a website and blog and we founded a fledgling professional learning network. I will discuss these briefly here and my fellow authors will refer to many of them in greater detail in the forthcoming chapters.

## *Professional learning groups*

Our establishment of professional learning groups came as part of an initiative from the Teaching Council of Ireland (see Teaching Council of Ireland 2012a). The Teaching Council of Ireland was interested in discovering how teachers could investigate their practice and seek to improve it using an action research approach. They asked us (authors) to investigate the viability of groups of teachers undertaking their own action research and to report on the process. We therefore established a small number of groups of teachers around Ireland who were interested in improving their practice and developing an action researcherly disposition. We also worked with whole-school teams of practitioners. The people who participated in these groups got no accreditation, time-in-lieu or extrinsic reward for taking part in the project; they were merely motivated by a desire to improve their own practice. We organized for these groups to meet up after school hours and we encouraged them to unearth their educational values as we discussed how they might approach undertaking an action research project in their workplace. These face-to-face meetings took place in the evenings, after work. Participants in these groups received guidance on establishing their educational values, help with critical reflection on their practice, encouragement to discuss their emerging ideas and solidarity in their efforts to improve practice. Many produced strong evidence and written reports on their projects and their learning from them.

We found these groups of teachers inspirational. Many attributed the changes and improvements to their practice – or the origins of the changes – to having opportunities to come together to share 'learning conversations' and being part of a community. We will discuss these professional learning groups in greater detail in later chapters.

## *Online CPD Programme*

Our next foray into establishing links with others who might be interested in learning about action research was to design and oversee an online professional development programme for teachers in Ireland on the basic principles of self-study action research. The programme, called *Enhancing Practice for Classroom Teachers*, was part of the continuous professional development (CPD) programme that primary school teachers in Ireland may undertake during their summer holidays, under the regulations of the Department of Education and Skills. These are commonly called 'Summer Courses' by primary teachers in Ireland. The teachers who participate in these programmes and complete all the requirements of it, receive a certificate of participation and recognition in terms of being awarded three personal leave days in the following school year. Our online course incorporated asynchronous participation in a discussion board and reflective commentary as compulsory aspects of participation. We ran revised versions of this programme for three consecutive summers, with a new cohort each year. We included exercises such as asking participants to articulate their educational values, reflect critically on their practice, read excerpts from the critical pedagogy theorists and share their critical reflections online on the discussion board with the community of teachers participating in the course, as well as with us. We authors acted as facilitators on the programme and we enjoyed engaging with the queries and conversations on the discussion boards.

The participants, in general, enjoyed the programme. Many made comments like these on the course:

It will be a huge challenge to take that step back from what Marian Dadds calls 'the hurry-along curriculum'. But with critical reflection the task will be easier … I was prompted to ask myself during the course: how can I do it better and why do I want to improve? But it is up to me to change me. Nevertheless I was happy to discover that I have been, for the most part, creating a democratic classroom where children are instrumental in their own learning. I endeavour to create a 'community of enquiry' in my classroom. I was reminded during the course about what a huge difference we as teachers make to people's lives. I must remember to not let my teaching life make a mockery of my teaching values. (Comment from one teacher on *Enhancing Practice for Classroom Teachers* Programme 2012)

For ourselves, we felt that we were working towards our own values as knowledge creators (Whitehead 2016) and making progress in our attempts to establish communities of action researchers. However, we also felt that using only a non-synchronous online platform was not the best way of exploring the complexities and nuances of self-study action research. While our programme gave a flavour of what engaging in self-study action research might 'feel' like for participants, we felt that its benefits were fleeting as each group only participated in the programme for the summer months and there was no opportunity to follow up on their learning once their summer programme was completed. We also felt that we were talking about self-study action research instead of experiencing it as a living process. However, a small number of participants did continue to engage with the action research process through our subsequent projects with communities of learners. We will discuss this in greater detail in Chapter 5.

## *Educational Action Research in Ireland (EARI)*

It seemed a natural progression for us to establish an online presence in terms of a static website initially, and then a blog space, to present and share our ideas and thoughts in a public forum. This web space can be accessed at http://www.eari.ie and is still 'live'. While our contributions to the blog are restricted by our own busy lives; time pressures and other commitments, it is helpful and energizing for us when people seek us out to make a comment, or email us regarding our input on the blog.

However, we found that our web space alone did not give that same sense of community; of dynamic discussion and engagement with the ideas that real, live face-to-face discussion can stimulate. It did not recreate the sense of dialogue that we experienced in our earlier years as we studied. We reminded ourselves that the purpose of dialogue, according to Bohm (Bohm and Peat 1987: 241), is 'to reveal the incoherence in our thought' so as to re-establish 'a creative collective consciousness'. We were not experiencing that creative collective consciousness, as the dialogue mainly flowed in just one direction – we wrote/spoke in our blog, but there was little or no response from those who read our ideas. Technically, this was not a dialogue in that there was no real flow of conversation in and between people. We needed to generate some form of dialogue, with at least a two-way flow, that would inspire us to think critically, question our assumptions, move our ideas on and provide us with an impetus for action.

## *Presentations, books and papers*

Throughout this time, we also produced a number of papers and books and also presented at various conferences. These can be found at www. eari.ie, under Research and Publications, and they explore various aspects of our understanding of action research. Very often we found that when we presented our work at conferences, we engaged in conversations with others. Occasionally we made friends for life at these events but usually the conversations were brief and just lasted for the day of the event. These were usually useful and interesting but rarely, if ever, did dialogue continue on into the future. They were missing Bohm's (2004) idea of 'flow' as outlined previously. Producing books and academic papers in the traditional manner hopefully informs and inspires readers but seldom instigates dialogue between readers and authors. However, should any reader wish to engage in an educational conversation with us about this or any other book or paper we have written, please contact us through our website at http://www.eari.ie

## *The Network of Educational Action Research in Ireland (NEARI)*

The newest and perhaps most successful version of our learning community is our current one. Drawing on the inspiration and energy of our colleague Pip Bruce Ferguson, we extended EARI (as outlined above) and generated NEARI: the Network of Educational Action Research in Ireland. Pip, who is from New Zealand, came to Ireland for a three-year placement in Dublin City University (DCU). When she arrived in Ireland, she needed to reach out to other action researchers and found it difficult to locate them. Eventually, we at EARI connected up with Pip and together we formed NEARI.

NEARI is the latest iteration of our learning community as we go to press and is, as yet, in its infancy. However, it is a growing movement and is gradually gaining momentum. It involves us (the four of us and Pip) and a group of people who are interested in action research. We have about three face-to-face meetings each year, at various venues in Ireland, with themes around action research and guest speakers, or round-robin sessions that are arranged in advance of each session. The gatherings are open to all who are interested in action research and in improving practice. Practitioners, students, lecturers and academics and anyone who is interested in exploring their practice and thinking in an action researcherly manner are all welcome to participate. NEARI is not aligned to any specific institution but moves from one venue to the next for each session and there is no membership fee. Participants have kindly 'donated' meeting facilities in their own various institutions and so there is no great need for funding at this stage. Whitaker et al. (2015) suggest that while they 'make a strong case for educators hoping to expand their knowledge ... and improve their practice by connecting' they suggest that no one 'vehicle' for communication can accomplish everything. At NEARI, we have developed multiple levels of communication, including an online discussion group. Topics of interest and burning questions are discussed in this arena between meetings and it provides a forum for people who are unable to attend. It also provides a connection with participants who want to remain silent but are listening. We have also included Skype in some of our meetings (see https://youtu.be/LSkwB4OJ9zE for example), and we have a Twitter handle @InfoNeari and use the hashtags #actionresearch and #NEARI. Whitaker et al. (2015: 8) explain the educational values of being connected on Twitter as inspiring us to 'expand your circle of professional colleagues outside your own organization to include others around the world who also desire to develop meaningful professional relationships'.

We must ask now if our learning community is becoming a personal learning network (PLN) for some of our participants. The following description of a PLN is from Lalande (2012):

> A Personal Learning Network is a way of describing the group of people that you connect with to learn their ideas, their questions, their reflections, and their references. Your PLN is not limited to online interactions, but it is that online, global interactive part that really makes it special. It is personal and you choose who's part of that group; you choose if you want to lurk – just check out what people are saying – or if you share; because you choose when to do so, and how to do so. (Lalande 2012: n.p.)

Contrary to Lalande's views, I believe that the 'online, global interactive part' is not what makes NEARI special. While the online interaction enhances the sense of connection and extends dialogue, it does not capture the essence of NEARI as a space for dialogue. However, NEARI is a new network and we cannot predict what shape it will have in the future, nor should we. Participants seem to enjoy the learning community as it stands at the moment and have commented thus at our face-to-face meetings:

> As someone who is still very early on in the action research journey, I found it very helpful and really appreciated the space to reflect and discuss issues with colleagues. (Feedback after NEARI meet, January 2016)
> We as a people (especially teachers) appear to have a fear around change and embracing new ideas. Almost afraid chaos will ensue. However, as you know the opposite occurs. So, stick with it, all the great ideas and

movements started slowly with a few key people. (Feedback after NEARI meet, January 2016)

Hurray! Can't wait for my brain's joyride! (Email, March 2016)

## 'Conveners' in a learning community

You can see in this chapter that many of the communities that we have described here emerged nearly intuitively for us. We had few aims apart from a wish to continue engaging in dialogue to support and extend learning. We had few rules or regulations apart from an acknowledgement of collegiality, support, mutual respect, safety and critical engagement. For many of us, our ultimate aim was to become better educators and to improve practice. However, Wenger-Trayner and Wenger-Trayner (2015: 99) use the term 'convener' to describe people who 'forge new learning partnerships'. Conveners are driven, like we are, by a conviction that 'new configurations of people and activities will bring about new capabilities' (ibid.) and unlock 'unexplored landscapes' (ibid.: 100). We consider ourselves to be invitational and welcoming but not coercive in our engagement with fellow NEARI participants. Wenger-Trayner and Wenger-Trayner (2015) also suggest that conveners learn to respect the role of boundaries and to move potential stakeholders or participants in the learning community beyond their current thinking and 'persuade them that coming across boundaries is worth their while' (ibid.). We, the authors, have had little persuading to do in our sixteen years of involvement in learning communities. We have however witnessed many participants meet with others on boundary 'fences', teeter on boundaries, cross boundaries and sometimes cross back again, and somehow even diminish boundaries. We have found that allowing the nature of our community to develop itself, without a heavy hand on the tiller, has been a successful model. Interestingly, Baker and Beames (2016) seem to support this idea, as they list 'No designated leadership positions, though significant leadership' and 'Not management-driven' (78) as being key elements in the success of a community of practice.

## To conclude

We have explored how sharing understanding and meanings with others in a learning community can help that community become a vibrant and sustainable place for learning. We have examined how we authors understand action research and outlined the close connections that we perceive exist between a community of practice and the action research process. The final sections of this chapter outline how we have extended and re-established learning communities since our initial foray into the learning community we described in Chapter 1.

We have come a long way from our beginnings as novice action researchers as we have continued on our learning journey. We may no longer communicate with one another using pen and paper but the spirit of connection remains the same, whether we meet face-to-face, online or by Skype. We are aware, as the 'conveners' of our learning community, that we do not know where our journey will lead. We know that once our community can sustain itself, we will have to let it go and allow it to grow and develop its own wings. As with all dialogue, the outcome will be unknown.

We are aware that, like Bohm (2004), there existed inherently in the various iterations of our learning communities the idea that there is a flow of meaning in the whole group and that new understandings may emerge. We remind ourselves frequently that these new meanings are 'the "glue" that holds people and societies together' (ibid.: 7) and we take our role in the formation of these groups seriously.

# 3

# Learning Communities as Sites of Transformation

## *Bernie Sullivan*

## Introduction

The idea of teachers immersing themselves in research projects that could result in improvement in their practice was not always presented as an option to members of the teaching profession. For many years there was an assumption that teachers had learned all that they needed to know about teaching and learning in their colleges of education or universities (Sugrue 1998). Thus, when they began their teaching careers, their role was defined in terms of teaching rather than learning, and so the need for cooperative initiatives with colleagues or for engaging in educational discourse was not widely recognized. The concept of lifelong learning had not yet gathered momentum among members of the teaching profession, and there did not appear to be any interest in undertaking further CPD. What we consider even more regrettable is the fact that teachers were regarded as lacking the capacity to engage in classroom research or to create knowledge from their own educational practice (Hiebert et al. 2002). Such a negative viewpoint has the potential to result ultimately in the systematic disempowerment of teachers and in a consequent diminishing of their status as educators. This is in sharp contrast with our perception of teachers as competent professionals, capable of undertaking research on their practice with the aim of improving it. In keeping with this view, and as outlined in Chapter 2, we authors became involved in setting up professional learning communities where teachers had the opportunity to bring about a transformation in their classroom practice and in their understanding of their practice, which is the subject matter of this chapter.

There are various opportunities currently available for teachers to become involved in professional learning communities. Teachers may wish to share their experiences of classroom practice with colleagues in an informal setting, or they might choose to engage in continuing professional development (CPD) courses provided by third-level colleges, teacher education centres, teachers' organizations or government education departments. Other teachers may decide to become involved in initial teacher education programmes, or they could opt to become mentors to newly qualified teachers. These initiatives have the potential to develop into effective learning communities, where participants have ample opportunities to cooperate and collaborate with one another, learn with and from one another and critically reflect on their thoughts and actions. In the process, teachers could learn much about their own educational practice and create significant new knowledge about their practice.

In this chapter, I will explore:

- our understanding of learning communities

- the functioning of an actual learning community

- the learning identified by participants in the learning community

- the learning that emerged for me from facilitating the group

- the transformative potential of a learning community

- how we can challenge the historic lack of incentive or opportunity for teachers to work collaboratively

- how to move towards more inclusive and democratic ways of working in classrooms.

## Our understanding of learning communities

It may be useful to explain briefly here what we authors understand by the term 'learning communities'. At the most basic level, we describe a learning community as a space where people with a common interest, such as achieving improvement in their educational practice, can come together to share their ideas; demonstrate values such as freedom, social justice, equality and inclusion; engage in dialogue and critical thinking; take responsibility for their own learning and begin to perceive themselves as knowledge creators. Evans et al. (2016) suggest that a community is not just a place to learn, but is also a source for learning and teaching. The ethos of cooperation and collaboration that prevails in a learning community contributes to the social dimension that adds coherence to the group. However, as Hiebert et al. (2002) point out, collaboration has a role beyond the mere socialization of the group – it also has a function in making public any new knowledge discovered during group discussions: 'Collaboration becomes essential for the development of professional knowledge, not only because collaboration provides teachers with social support groups but because collaborations force their participants to make their knowledge public and understood by colleagues' (7). The idea of sharing new knowledge by making it public is central to the work of Hiebert et al. (2002) who suggest that it could contribute to creating a knowledge base for the teaching profession. Effective learning communities may exhibit characteristics such as the unbridled sharing of values, ideas and resources; a strong focus on working as a group rather than solely on an individual basis; and engagement in dialogue and critical discourse with the potential to result in the creation of new knowledge, as Máirín discussed in Chapter 1. I will provide a practical example of a learning community of teachers, which I facilitated, following the opportunity for reflection below.

## Reflective opportunity

Why do you think it might be important for teachers to cooperate and collaborate with one another?
What are the advantages of engaging in dialogue with colleagues?
What might be the benefits for students in schools where their teachers work collaboratively with colleagues?

## The functioning of an actual learning community

We authors became involved in setting up learning communities for teachers as a result of an initiative supported by the Teaching Council of Ireland in 2011/2. We were convinced of the potential of self-study action research as a methodology through which teachers could engage in CPD, as Máirín outlined earlier. We were firmly committed to the idea of lifelong learning, as evidenced by: our studies for MA and PhD degrees, our presentations at various education conferences, our writing for refereed journals and our co-authored books (McDonagh et al. 2012; Sullivan et al. 2016). We believed that teachers could be powerful agents of change in their own classrooms, and that they could bring about effective improvement through critically reflecting on their practice. Through their engagement with this process, teachers could experience a sense of self-empowerment as they took responsibility for their own learning and for the creation of new knowledge of their educational practice. Niemi et al. (2012) point out that this approach would require a change from professional development delivered to teachers, to a situation where teachers are developing their own professional learning in relation to their particular classroom context. In a project aimed at the realization of this ideology, and also conscious of the prospect of achieving the fulfilment of our commitments as outlined above, we envisaged the setting up of learning communities of interested teachers whom we would support by providing them with the framework for a self-study action research approach to evaluating their practice for the purpose of improving it. We put our proposal to the Teaching Council and, convinced of its viability as a valid form of CPD, the council agreed to commission the project (Teaching Council of Ireland 2012a).

To set our project in motion, we issued invitations to teachers who might wish to participate in our undertaking, by advertising in Teacher Education Centres and contacting school principals who were known to us. Consequently, some of the learning communities with whom we worked were located in Teacher Education Centres and consisted of teachers from a variety of schools and across all levels – primary, post-primary and third-level. Other groups comprised whole-school staffs and took place in the respective schools: these were all primary schools. I will now focus on a group that formed in an Education Centre, and that I facilitated, as I describe and explain how the learning community offered a collaborative and dialogical space for teachers to explore, interrogate, critique and seek solutions to issues of concern to them in their daily classroom practice.

### Example of a learning community

The participants in the project included primary and post-primary teachers, both male and female. Many of the teachers taught in schools in disadvantaged areas, while one teacher taught in a private school. One of the primary school teachers worked in the area of learning support, and one of the post-primary teachers, who was deaf, taught in a school for girls who were deaf. The group, then, was quite diverse and covered a broad spectrum of educational situations. At the initial meeting, I outlined the purpose of the project to the teachers and gave a brief explanation of the principles of self-study action research, and of what utilizing this approach entailed for them. I explained that the project would last for six months, with face-to-face meetings taking place monthly, and with the option of also engaging in online discussions as a means of further support for participants. My aim was that, by the end of the six-month period, the teachers would have carried out a self-study action research assignment on their classroom practice for the purpose of improving their practice or their understanding of it. From the beginning, the teachers displayed an enthusiasm for the project, as they began to engage in dialogue with one another about the task that I had suggested they might undertake before our next meeting: to identify an area of practice that they wished to change, and to explain why they wished to make the proposed change.

The research topics that teachers brought to the second meeting were wide-ranging and individualized, reflecting each teacher's particular concern. It is worth including some of the research questions here, to indicate the variety of concerns that they had about their practice:

- How can I ensure whole-staff involvement in the green flag environmental initiative?

- How can I become more organized so that weekly plans are completed?

- As a learning support teacher, how can I ensure that a pupil with dyslexia is included in mainstream class activities?

- How can I use ICT to meet the needs of both aural and visual learners?

From their answers as to why they wanted to research their identified topics, it became evident that the teachers wished to improve an area of their practice that was not commensurate with their educational values. As values are kernel to a self-study action research approach, I used this opportunity for the teachers to articulate their educational values, and for a discussion on the idea of experiencing oneself as a living contradiction, which occurs when one's values are not being realized in one's practice (Whitehead 1989; 1993; 2000; 2015). The notion of linking the concerns that teachers had with the denial of their educational values in their practice was a new experience for the teachers. An awareness of the tensions that this situation can lead to, and the compulsion that teachers may feel to try to resolve the contradiction, contributed to an enhanced understanding of their practice and of how they could bring about improvement in it.

As each teacher described their current situation, and how they wished to change it to one that would reflect working towards improvement, other members of the group gave advice or made suggestions that either had worked for them or that they felt could ameliorate the situation.

This atmosphere of collegiality, cooperation and collaboration set the tone for the remainder of the project. We authors had experienced the transformative nature of this way of working with one another when we were undertaking research for our PhD degrees, as Máirín described in Chapter 1. It was uplifting to witness the embodiment of collaborative and dialogical values in the participants' interactions. This echoes the views of Hiebert et al. (2002: 7) in relation to the benefits of attending to the nature and quality of approach in a learning community, to ensure that it is collaborative and dialogical: 'Collaboration – a process considered central to successful professional development programs – ensures that what is discovered will be communicable because it is discovered in the context of group discussion.'

At each meeting, participants outlined how their research project was progressing, and their colleagues provided feedback and made recommendations for further progress. I, as facilitator, provided the structure of the programme, advising the teachers on areas such as data gathering, accessing relevant literature and identifying their educational values. Based on my own experiences of undertaking action research, I recommended that the teachers should keep a reflective journal, in which they would record details of their project as it unfolded, as well as their critical reflections on the process (Sullivan et al. 2016). I also ensured that the project was conducted within a framework of equality and inclusion, through engaging in strategies that allowed all participants equal opportunity to have their voices heard, thus avoiding a situation where one dominant voice might hold sway.

I have described the group that I supported, as its members undertook research on their practice, as a learning community. I have demonstrated how the group met the requirements needed in order to be designated as a community: equality of participation, ethos of cooperation and collaboration, opportunity for dialogue and discourse and shared commitment to achieving improvement in practice. Where then, you may ask, was the learning element, and what evidence do you have that learning occurred? I suggest that the learning occurred at two different levels: the teachers who participated in the group provided feedback on their learning from engaging with the process, and I also identified my learning from my action research on my experience of facilitating the learning community. The duality of the learning experience that can occur is mentioned by Lewis and Allan (2005: 6) as a characteristic of dynamic learning communities: 'In learning communities members share control and everyone learns, including the facilitator or tutor or group leader.' I outline below the main learning from the perspective of the participating teachers and from my perspective as facilitator.

# Reflective opportunity

How might an action research approach be a suitable framework for organizing a learning community?

What advantages do you think you might gain from participating in a learning community?

What could you learn from keeping a reflective journal?

# Learning identified by participants in the learning community

At the end of the six-month period, the teachers were asked to evaluate their experiences of participating in the action research project. To provide evidence of participants' learning, I will focus on three of the questions that were included in the evaluation forms. The three questions are:

1. Do you feel that you have improved your understanding, your learning or your relationships with colleagues or with students?

2. Has participation in the project changed you as a teacher? How?

3. What has been the most significant learning for you from this project?

My reason for choosing these particular questions was that they focused specifically on the teachers' own learning from participating in the project, and on any changes that occurred, in themselves or in their practice, during the course of their research. The learning identified by the participants is significant because it reflects three different areas of educational practice: cultivating a learning environment that is more student-oriented than teacher-focused, identifying the diverse learning requirements of students in order to be able to adjust the teaching approach and the importance of developing respectful professional relationships with colleagues.

1. In answer to the question as to whether they felt they had achieved improvement in any area of their practice, participants outlined the various ways that they could discern improvement, whether in their own teaching practice, in their students' learning or in their professional relationships with colleagues. This is the response from one participant, who was convinced that improvement had occurred:

This approach has enabled me to improve on becoming a better teacher as I implement a more student-oriented learning environment than an approach where the teacher is doing too much talking. (Feedback A, June 2011)

Another participant identified the improvement in her learning in relation to how she felt compelled to take into account the diverse learning styles of her students:

> I became more critical of my own practices. I had to find the style of learning that my pupils used and adapt my lessons to ensure all children's learning styles/needs were catered for within my lesson, as I discovered in the past my lessons had mainly been suited for visual learners as that is my own style of learning. (Feedback B, June 2011)

A learning support teacher who withdrew students from their mainstream classes to provide them with extra learning support, mentioned that her relationship with a mainstream class teacher had improved:

> There was always mutual respect between the class teacher and myself but it was enhanced and cemented. I'm not sure that this relationship would be possible with every staff member. There can sometimes be a culture of competition. (Feedback C, June 2011)

I suggest that these are significant learning outcomes for the participants who engaged in the six-month project and that the outcomes represent an improvement in their practice, as they have claimed.

2. The second question required teachers to comment on whether participating in the project had changed them as teachers, and in what way. The various ways in which they felt their teaching lives had changed included: an initial shift in focus to individual students' needs in one pedagogic area beginning to impact on other areas of practice, recognizing the value of keeping a reflective journal and of taking cognizance of colleagues' views and using reflection to aid planning and so become more effective and more efficient in their professional lives. One participant's response to question two was:

> Yes, I am more focused on the individual needs within my class.... I have found that by tackling and improving this one area of my teaching, there has been a positive knock-on effect in other areas of my teaching. (Feedback D, June 2011)

Another teacher felt that one of the things that contributed to changing her as a teacher was the keeping of a reflective journal, which I had recommended at the outset of the project, and also her more frequent interactions with other staff members:

> The journal has offered an extra way of evaluating my own work. I also bounce ideas off others more often and consider the 'off-the-cuff' remarks

of another staff member more seriously. At times, someone outside can help me see a situation from another angle. (Feedback E, June 2011)

The use of a reflective journal was also mentioned by another participant, who described his use of it as being effective in bringing about a change in his teaching, and in ensuring that he became more efficient in lesson planning:

I personally enjoyed the focus on my own teaching and learning, from month to month, and the journal for me was very rewarding, as it gave me good reason to reflect on my teaching, as well as plan more effectively and efficiently for the following month's teaching, as well as for our group meeting. (Feedback F, June 2011)

I found it heartening, and at the same time humbling, to read of the changes that teachers identified as occurring in their professional lives through undertaking their action research projects in the learning community that I had facilitated.

3. As the data below shows, each teacher articulated with confidence and clarity the significance for them of undertaking their action research projects. The change in their understanding of their practice was important to them as they could see the impact of their improved understanding on other aspects of teaching and learning. Teachers displayed the self-confidence and self-efficacy to regard themselves as competent knowledge creators and as being just as capable as external experts in understanding their own practice. In relation to the most significant learning that resulted from undertaking the action research project, one teacher wrote:

I think that the most significant learning I got from this project is understanding what I am doing more thoroughly and understanding that I can improve it. The challenging part is figuring out 'How can I improve it?' (Feedback G, June 2011)

Another participant found that for her, the most significant learning arose from the activity of reflecting constantly and critically on her practice, as she describes here:

I have learned that it is important to reflect on my teaching style as in time we can become set in our ways, and that by changing one aspect of my teaching, the quality of my deliverance, and the children's learning and achievements, has greatly improved. (Feedback H, June 2011)

The response of a third teacher to this question demonstrates that she had progressed from a view that perceives knowledge creation as being the prerogative of the academic to now understanding that her practitioner knowledge also has value. This is her description of the significance of this understanding:

> I seek expert/academic knowledge to apply sound principles to specific situations, but improvement lies within my understanding of the situation. I should act on the evidence in front of me to help improve the learning of a given child. No expert has been faced with exactly this task. (Feedback I, June 2011)

In the learning community, these empowering and inspiring views on teaching and learning were shared with all members and discussed in an open and collaborative forum. In this context, the teachers were contributing to the knowledge base of the teaching profession (Hiebert et al. 2002) and perceiving themselves as knowledge creators (Whitehead 2016).

## The learning that emerged for me from facilitating the group

My aim in setting up the group was to share my passion and enthusiasm for action research and introduce teachers to the idea that they were knowledge creators who had ownership of their own learning, as they engaged in researching their practice within a learning community. I also wished to research my role as I participated in, and facilitated, the group in carrying out their projects, while acknowledging values around empowerment and knowledge creation, and without impinging on the sense of agency and self-efficacy of the members. My role, apart from my initial input on the principles and practice of action research, consisted in inviting suggestions from other members of our group, who all contributed feedback, ideas and comments throughout the process. However, at times I also needed to adopt a more active leadership role as regards ensuring that participants remained focused and that the momentum continued for the duration of the project.

One of the main learning outcomes for me was the realization that a group of teachers from diverse backgrounds in education could blend into a vibrant and successful learning community. The teachers had been transformed from an initial collection of 'I's to a collective 'we' (Sergiovanni 1994) through constructive dialogue. This does not mean that groupthink, or an attempt to reach consensus, was involved but that each member had the opportunity to contribute to the dialogue and the knowledge creation. In the process, an ethos of equity prevailed and this diminished the prospect of adverse power relations (Foucault 1980b). The diversity of concerns that teachers brought to the group, and which they formed into their research topics, did not prove to be a barrier to the cohesion of the group. On the contrary, the opportunity to highlight issues of concern and to have them discussed, teased out and critiqued by the other participants, whose professional expertise and personal insights produced a broad panoply of opinions on the issues, resulted in a close bond of solidarity and interconnectedness. An example of the spirit of cooperation and collaboration that characterized the group occurred when one teacher, who prior to participating in the learning community had focused almost exclusively on completing the mathematic curriculum as she struggled to prepare students for state examinations, was encouraged by the other members of the group to change to a more student-centred approach, with a strong emphasis on students' understanding of mathematical concepts. The teacher's success in implementing this strategy prompted her to claim, at the end of the project, 'My teaching has become more innovative and has established a student-oriented learning environment.' I suggest that the change in this teacher's approach represents a significant transformation in her thinking and in her practice.

Facilitating the group enabled me to realize that size matters in such undertakings. If a group is too large, it may result in an extra challenge for facilitators as they try to ensure that everyone is afforded an opportunity to contribute to discussions. Because our group was small in number, each participant had ample time to express an opinion, or to request feedback or advice, at each meeting. Some of the teachers in the learning community mentioned in their evaluations that the smallness of the group was a positive factor for them. One teacher wrote, 'I loved the small group as it afforded everybody ample time to present and share their ideas, concerns and successes', while another stated, 'I think it was useful to meet in small groups as we did, where you could share your findings and seek advice from others.' Lewis and Allan (2005: 10) share the view that small groups can be more effective, noting among the advantages that 'the group should be small enough for members to form relationships and get to know each other well'.

A significant learning outcome for me was the fact that a group of teachers, who initially articulated their concerns as problems that might not be resolved easily, succeeded in making considerable progress in bringing about changes in their situations through their participation in the learning community. Once the impetus to try to bring about improvement in practice had become an acceptable and possible prospect for the teachers, the motivation to persevere with the project was sustained through the cooperation and collaboration of colleagues. The commitment, dedication and work ethic of the teachers ensured that they persisted with the project until its conclusion, and that each teacher experienced a measure of success within the relatively short timeframe of the project. One of the participants articulated her positive experience and her wish to continue using action research as a means of improvement when she wrote, 'I really got a lot out of it and will continue with my action research this year as I try to incorporate the use of iPads into my lessons.' Another participant successfully submitted a proposal, based on her research during the project, to study for a master's degree. It was also a significant outcome for me that a teacher asked if I would undertake a whole-school action research project with staff in her school during the coming school year.

Lest it might appear that I am presenting a victory narrative (MacLure 1996), I will refer here to some recommendations made by participants in their evaluations. I mentioned earlier in the chapter that I perceived the diversity of education situations reflected in the learning community as a positive factor, providing as it did a wide range of perspectives. However, one teacher did not regard the participation of teachers from different levels in education as an advantage. He felt that it would have been much more beneficial for him if he had been in a group consisting of primary school teachers only, as they would have had a shared interest in terms of students' ages, curriculum subjects and timetabling issues. This was a valid point, as there were occasions where I had to clarify some aspects of the primary school situation for the post-primary teachers and vice versa, a matter that did not arise when we subsequently worked with a whole-school staff in a primary school, which Caitriona describes in Chapter 7. Nevertheless, I thought that the contributions of the post-primary teachers added much to our discussions and provided another dimension that broadened the range of perspectives available. Another participant concurred with my view that it was beneficial to have different viewpoints, and wrote in her evaluation, 'It was nice to have a mix of all areas of the teaching profession – primary, post-primary, learning support etc.' There was a further recommendation from a teacher to the effect that he would have preferred if the course had been coterminous with the school year. This in fact had been my initial intention, but it had taken longer than I had anticipated to get the project up and running, and so it was almost three months into the school year when I began. If I were to undertake a similar project again, I would ensure that it would start at the beginning of the school year.

# Reflective opportunity

The teachers all participated in the same learning community, yet identified different learning outcomes. What do you feel is the significance of this?

How important is it that all the teachers were able to describe changes in their professional practice?

What part, do you think, did teachers' critical reflection play in bringing about change?

# The transformative potential of a learning community

We authors are convinced of the power of learning communities to bring about a transformation in the professional lives of participants who engage wholeheartedly with the process. In the example that I outlined in this chapter, it is evident that each teacher made significant progress in relation to achieving improvement in some aspect of their teaching practice or their understanding of it. Teachers have explained how their learning was enhanced through participating in the learning community, and many of the participants described how their students also benefited from it. I suggest that the self-study action research approach that I used as a framework for the project was instrumental in bringing about much of the learning that occurred. This methodology ensured that the focus was on the self, as each individual worked on changing their own attitude, thinking or pedagogic approach, which in some cases produced a knock-on effect in terms of improvement in the learning of their students or of having an educational influence in the learning of their colleagues.

The learning that teachers gained through participating in the learning community is of major significance, as it represents new knowledge created by them. Through engaging in constructive dialogue with one another, providing critical feedback and making suggestions when appropriate, teachers produced new meanings and new understandings of their work. In this process, they were in reality creating new knowledge about their practice – I gave some examples of the knowledge they created earlier in this chapter. Lewis and Allan (2005: 12) acknowledge the potential for epistemological enhancement through participating in learning communities, when they explain how an individual's personal knowledge becomes explicit through sharing it with the group: 'In many respects learning communities are concerned with explicit knowledge and also the codification of tacit knowledge into explicit knowledge. The process of transforming tacit into explicit knowledge is a key activity of learning communities.' The significance of this epistemological phenomenon lies in the fact that, in the traditional view, teachers were not regarded as competent researchers or as potential developers of new knowledge of their practice. In this chapter, I provided evidence that practising teachers can be creators of knowledge through self-reflection on their actions and on their thinking, and through articulating their learning from their reflections. Evans et al. (2016: 10) appear to accept the view that knowledge creation is a natural outcome of participation in a learning community: 'Community is a place where people are creating knowledge about the community and about themselves.'

I suggest that the teachers who participated in the learning community developed a theory of their practice through articulating their new knowledge that evolved from carrying out their research projects, having gathered data and presented evidence of their findings to other members of the group for validation. For example, one participant wrote of how she realized the importance of reflecting on her teaching style, as I quoted earlier. She was then able to articulate her theory of practice that by changing just one aspect of her teaching, the quality of her practice and the children's learning had improved significantly. Another teacher developed a theory in relation to her practice that she should act on the evidence in front of her, and on her understanding of the situation, rather than only looking to theorists or academics for the knowledge to bring about improvement in her students' learning. For a third teacher, the theory that evolved from her new knowledge and learning about her practice concerned her deeper understanding of her practice – understanding what she was doing more thoroughly and understanding that she could improve the situation.

The theory-creating achievements of the teachers, emanating from their self-study action research, represented a significant transformation in their practice. Teachers demonstrated their ability to undertake research, collect data and identify findings, whilst critically reflecting on the process throughout. They are practitioners, working in classroom situations where they are confronted with a variety of problems, difficulties and conflicting narratives on a daily basis. Their efforts to bring about improvement in their situations, through implementing change and attempting to live their educational values in their practice, resulted in the articulation of new knowledge and new theories of their practice. The teachers did not experience any dichotomy in their roles as practitioners and, simultaneously, knowledge creators. As a facilitator of their research process, I did not perceive any contradiction in their joint roles either. This is a particularly significant outcome, given that there has long existed in educational discourse a distinct division between theory and practice that promotes a view of the academic as having responsibility for the creation of theory while the role of the teachers is to implement that theory in their practice. As Hiebert et al. (2002: 11) state, 'Professional knowledge building became the province of researchers, applying the knowledge was left to the practitioners.' In agreement with Giroux (2011), Kincheloe (2003), Nias (1989) and Schön (1995), among others, I subscribe to the view that teachers can develop theories of practice through undertaking research on their practice.

I have provided the evidence to support this viewpoint in the preceding paragraphs, where teachers occupied hybrid spaces as they combined theory and practice in their research projects. The teachers, then, could be regarded as professionals who straddled the gap between theory and practice, which we authors consider to be a significant and innovative achievement.

Participating in the learning community proved to be an effective form of CPD for the teachers involved. The fact that it occurred during school term meant that teachers could implement their plans immediately in their educational practice and monitor the changes to ascertain whether there had been an improvement. When CPD is provided during school holiday time, the momentum and the motivation to engage with the concepts presented, or to try out any new ideas, can be significantly reduced by the time teachers have returned to the classroom. It was also significant that teachers attended the meetings of their own volition. There was no compulsion on them to participate: they were there in response to an open invitation and on foot of their own decision. Neither was there any incentive for them to take part: there was no monetary gain, no academic qualification and no days-in-lieu. The sole motivation was the teachers' personal commitment to improving their own professional lives and their students' educational experiences.

I found it uplifting to note the candour and sincerity with which the teachers examined their practice in order to identify an area for improvement. It is not easy to admit to oneself, or to others, that there may be an area of professional practice that is not commensurate with one's educational values: yet, the participants embraced with openness and honesty the opportunity to interrogate, and implement change in, their practice for the betterment of both themselves and their students. Dadds and Hart (2001) suggest that opening up one's practice to critical scrutiny in this manner demands courage and fortitude, as well as a willingness to accept that there are always opportunities for further development. They also feel that it can leave one in a vulnerable position when faced with critique, whether from self or from others, but that the outcomes often justify the investment of self: 'It often means that the practitioner researcher renders himself or herself open to critique, from both self and others. Yet such open attitudes, we believe, signal one of the highest forms of professionalism. Such professionalism deserves fostering and respecting in climates of optimum growth' (ibid.: 9).

# Reflective opportunity

How might participation in a learning community achieve transformation in your teaching practice?

What might be the significance for you of any new learning about your
practice?
How might you develop your potential as a knowledge creator?

# Challenging the historic lack of incentive or opportunity for collaboration among teachers

In setting up the learning community that I have described above, I was
motivated by a desire to change a situation that had existed for many years,
whereby teachers worked for the most part in isolation in their classrooms
(Ball 2003; Goodlad 1984; Lieberman 1988; Lortie 1975). There was little
interaction with other teachers on educational matters, and therefore little
opportunity to share good ideas, celebrate any successes, interrogate
reasons for failures, discuss possibilities for future initiatives or critique
pedagogic approaches. Some schools became places where a culture of
individualism thrived and where teachers, unwittingly or otherwise, found
themselves enmeshed in an atmosphere of competitiveness as they felt
compelled to focus on achieving the highest possible test scores for their
students. Hargreaves (1992: 232) believes that the culture of individualism is
pervasive and that 'it isolates teachers from their colleagues and ties them to
the pressing immediacy of classroom life'. Evans et al. (2016: 2) suggest that
there is a distinct link between the practice of individualism and the ethos of
competitiveness that currently characterizes many schools: 'We know that
individualism is devoted toward competition and to the notions that teachers
should have the ability to build up a "useful" knowledge and skills, which
should be related directly to competition in the labour market.'

In such a scenario of individualism and competitiveness, many teachers
found themselves locked into a system that evaluated their expertise in
teaching in relation to how well their students performed in standardized
tests. Constrained by the pressures of such an approach, teachers were
unlikely to encourage their students to engage in cooperative strategies,
or to scaffold one another in their learning endeavours. Savin-Baden and
Major (2004) suggest that the culture of individualism that is often prevalent
and promoted worldwide is causing difficulties for team-based learning
approaches. It is hardly surprising, therefore, that teachers did not always
recognize the need for collegiality, for critical dialogue with peers or for
engaging in CPD to enhance their professional lives. This situation reflects
my personal experience of the ethos that prevailed in many schools at the

beginning of my teaching career. I recall teachers going into their classrooms when they arrived in school each morning and remaining there, apart from going to the staffroom for lunch break, until school finished in the afternoon. The conversations at lunch break centred mainly on teachers' social lives or on their families: on the rare occasions when school featured as a topic, it was usually in relation to class management issues or anecdotes from teachers' classrooms.

The necessity for teachers to engage in CPD in order to be able to meet the challenges that arise during their careers is articulated as follows by Livingston (2012: 36): 'Teachers have an ongoing commitment to maintain their professional expertise and must recognise themselves as learners.' She advocates that teachers need to continually revise and enhance their knowledge and skills as well as their teaching and learning approaches. However, the provision of CPD has often been haphazard and piecemeal, and has been imposed on teachers by external providers, rather than emanating from teachers' actual, real-life and practical experience, or from teachers' own awareness of their felt needs in this area. Garet et al. (2001: 927) critique the lack of cohesion in much of the professional development provided for teachers: 'Professional development for teachers is frequently criticized on the ground that the activities are disconnected from one another – in other words, individual activities do not form part of a coherent program of teacher learning and development.'

A report from the OECD (2005: 122) claims that 'professional development is often fragmented, unrelated to teaching practice and lacking in intensity and follow-up'. Attention needs to be paid, therefore, to the quality of CPD offered to teachers, if it is to be effective, long-term and coherent: teachers should feel that they have ownership of the process, it should continue throughout their professional careers, it should be based on principles of cooperation and collaboration and it should reflect an improvement in their learning as well as in the learning of their students. Livingston (2012: 40) endorses this view: 'Rather than experiencing professional development activities as a collection of separate, sporadic, random or abstract activities, teachers themselves should be supported and encouraged to have ownership and continually build on and extend and deepen their own learning in a proactive and progressive way throughout their careers.' I suggest that the self-study action research approach, which I used in the learning community that I facilitated, not only fulfilled many of the requirements for quality CPD as outlined here, but went beyond this in providing teachers with the opportunity to think critically about their practice, to examine the values that shaped their professional lives and to bring about a transformation in their practice through reflection and action.

# A move towards more inclusive and democratic ways of working in the classroom

Gradually, a change has been taking place in the situation I described above. The focus is now shifting towards teachers sharing their experiences of classroom practice, and learning with and from each other. Fitzallen and Brown (2016: 7) claim that there is a move away from research carried out only by external researchers, and that 'inquiries by teachers themselves are gaining traction'. Teachers are being encouraged to develop more inclusive ways of working that could enhance teaching and learning both for themselves and for their students. As a result, there are increasing instances of staffrooms becoming sites for professional conversations that could lead to the enrichment of the educational experience for all participants. The ethos of individualism is now being replaced by principles of cooperation and collaboration that could contribute to a more positive and life-enhancing experience of education for teachers and students. However, achieving this change in culture is not a straightforward or facile task, as indicated by Humada-Ludeke (2013: 21) who, in relation to the need for school leaders to engage in a paradigm shift in order to transform school cultures, suggests that 'the school moves from a culture of deep ingrained isolated practices to a culture of collaboration which requires shared-practice, transparency, trust, a collective sense of purpose, and a team of professionals who value continuous learning'.

The move towards more inclusive and more democratic educational practices, and the ethos of cooperation and collaboration that this is engendering, has resulted in many teachers focusing more on their own learning and on sharing that learning with colleagues. There is a greater emphasis on communication as teachers share ideas, methodologies and pedagogic strategies with one another. A new culture of dialogue and discourse is gradually replacing the former sense of isolation and disconnectedness that characterized many classroom situations and left teachers often feeling that they had no access to the support, care, advice or expertise of colleagues. The introduction of school self-evaluation into many education systems across the globe has encouraged some teachers to engage in self-reflection as they critically evaluate their practice (Ireland, Department of Education and Skills 2012a and 2012b; UK, Department for Education and Skills 2004). However, if the self-evaluation is imposed on the teachers, rather than undertaken of their own free will, there is a danger that the process could lack rigour and remain at a superficial level. Nevertheless, where there is genuine self-reflection, the changing circumstances in which teachers now find themselves could be described as embryonic learning communities, which, given time, space and opportunity, could develop into powerful sites of possibility, dialogue and progress in promoting educational discourse and practices. Hiebert et al. (2002: 3) attest to the benefits of changing to more collaborative work practices: 'Teachers, who traditionally have worked in isolation, report favorably on programs that bring them in close contact with colleagues in active work on improving practice.' It would appear, therefore, that learning communities could provide the space and opportunity for teachers to engage in meaningful and critical reflection and evaluation of their practice, and that they might best achieve this through supportive and collaborative partnerships with colleagues.

# To conclude

In this chapter, I described how I set up a learning community of teachers who used a self-study action research approach as they reflected on their practice, took action to implement change and created new learning and new theories of their practice. I put forward compelling arguments for the view that CPD for teachers can be effectively and efficiently achieved through participating in learning communities that can provide opportunities for professional conversations, and engaging in a self-study action research methodology to bring about improvement in their practice or their understanding of it. This approach is underpinned by ontological values of social justice, inclusion and democracy; epistemological values of dialogue, communication and knowledge creation; and educational values of cooperation and collaboration. I outlined the learning identified by the participants who undertook research on their practice and also my learning from my experience in supporting the group. I indicated how the new knowledge created by the teachers could be articulated as their personal theories of practice, and how each of them effected a transformational change in their practice. In the process, they achieved a phenomenon that belied the traditional separation of theory and practice, a topic to which I will return in the next chapter.

# 4

# A Theoretical Explanation of the Practical Significance of Learning Communities

## Bernie Sullivan

## Introduction

When teachers participate in learning communities, they are enabling the possibility of developing strong and robust partnerships, as well as assisting in the creation of new knowledge of educational import. The partnerships in which teachers participate may be school-based initiatives with colleagues, they may be collaborative undertakings with teachers from other schools or they may be school/university enterprises. Each of these has the potential to contribute significantly to the betterment of teaching and learning for the participants and for their students. I described in the previous chapter how a random group of teachers from varying educational backgrounds formed a learning community and, through a process of critical reflection and action, succeeded in achieving improvement in their practice and in their understanding of their practice. The cooperative and collaborative approach that framed the participating teachers' research projects was instrumental in effecting a transformation in their teaching practice and in facilitating their articulation of the significance of their resultant learning. I now focus on the theoretical underpinnings of learning communities and examine how learning communities can be influential in the efforts to combine theory and practice in classroom-based research. I offer explanations for the prospect that allowing teachers to have more control over their own professional development, through engaging in self-study action research, has the potential to achieve significant improvement in their practice.

In this chapter I explore:

- the traditional separation of theory and practice

- some of the reasons for this dichotomy

- various efforts made to reconcile theory and practice

- the influence of critical pedagogy

- how to bridge the gap between practitioner and academic knowledge

- the role of learning communities in combining theory and practice

- how learning communities can act as models for classroom interactions.

# Separation of theory and practice

Traditionally, there has existed in educational parlance a distinct division between theory and practice (Hiebert et al. 2002), and a corresponding separation of the roles of academic and practitioner. This division has been sustained by a form of questionable thinking that promotes a hierarchical structure within the various levels of the education system (Schön 1995). According to this particular logic, academics in universities and colleges of education were considered to be eminently qualified for the task of creating knowledge and developing theory. In contrast, classroom teachers were seen as practitioners who were best suited to implementing, or testing in their practice, the theories developed for them by the academics. This unequal situation of dualism between academic and practitioner, theory and practice, prompted MacLure (1996: 282) to critique 'the tyrannies that theory and expertise have exerted upon the teacher as the Other'. She suggests the need for exploring alternative approaches 'as ways of freeing teachers and researchers from the oppressive certainties of theory' (ibid.).

It was generally accepted that teachers were not capable of engaging in the difficult and challenging task of developing theory, since they were working at the supposedly lower level of classroom practice, rather than in the higher echelons of third level institutions. The abstract theory of the academics was regarded as of far greater significance than the practical knowledge of classroom teachers. Teachers could, of course, support academic researchers in their work, for example by allowing their classrooms to be used for research purposes, by collecting data for the researchers or by providing feedback, but their role was very much a subsidiary one. Schön (1995) describes the above situation by using a metaphor in which the academics inhabit the lofty highlands of theory, while practitioners toil away in the swampy lowlands of practice: 'In the varied topography of professional practice, there is a high, hard ground overlooking a swamp. On the high ground, manageable problems lend themselves to solution through the use of research-based theory and technique. In the swampy lowlands, problems are messy and confusing and incapable of technical solution' (ibid.: 28). Schön (ibid.) goes on to suggest that the problems at the level of the high ground may have little relevance for society at large, whereas the problems encountered at the level of the swamp tend to be of the greatest human concern. However, it is those working at the theoretical level of the high ground who are held in the highest regard, while those working in the swampy lowlands of practice are seen as somewhat inferior to the theorists and academics.

When such hierarchical structures are deeply embedded in education systems, it can prove extremely difficult to dismantle them, or perhaps even to challenge them or question their validity and authenticity. Nias (1989: 171) argues that the hierarchical nature of many schools and education systems encourages belief in 'two largely unchallenged assumptions about knowledge: that those in authority possess it and that learning therefore passes downward'. This top-down approach to knowledge has dominated epistemological discourse for far too long, and so perhaps it is time to find an alternative format, or to try to lessen the effect of its domination by consciously and constructively engaging in a bottom-up approach that would ensure greater equality for all. Kincheloe (2003) articulates some of the problematics associated with a top-down approach to knowledge creation when he argues that when teachers are seen as receivers rather than producers of knowledge, there occurs a deskilling of teachers and a dumbing-down of curriculum. I suggest that in view of such demeaning and patronizing effects, there is a strong rationale for disrupting the status quo in relation to knowledge creation. With this purpose in mind, we authors aimed to establish learning communities that eschewed top-down approaches and embraced socially constructed ways of coming to know, an example of which I outlined in Chapter 3, where teachers became knowledge creators as they embraced the challenges of the swampy lowlands of their daily practice.

The current global tendency to apply a business model to educational institutions, and to consider that the sole purpose of education is to prepare students for the job market, could deprive students of the opportunity for critical thinking and for knowledge creation, thus contributing to the continuous separation of theory and practice. Paraskeva (2015) ascribes this stance to the culture of anti-intellectualism that is often directed towards teachers and schools. He suggests that proponents of this form of thinking, who often subscribe to neoliberal ideologies, do not accept that teachers can be creators of knowledge in their practice. In agreement with Giroux (2011), he critiques the view that does not recognize that 'teachers might actually be educated as critical intellectuals – thoroughly versed in theory and subject matter and not simply methods – and might engage in the dangerous practice of teaching students how to think, hold power and authority accountable, take risks, and willingly embrace their role as producers of knowledge and not merely transmitters of information' (xvii). Similarly, McLaren (2015: 20) decries the trend towards neoliberal consumerism that frames much of the theory and practice in education, and argues for the need 'to challenge the proponents of the competitive market whose corporate outlawry is driving the reform initiatives of education today'. He warns that, in succumbing to the all-pervasive influence of corporations that try to mould us to their desired shape, 'we have become a less mindful, less vigilant citizenry, watching passively as civil life becomes swallowed up by the logic of capital, consumption and corporatism' (ibid.: 140). I believe that we can counteract any negative impact from external sources of influence through establishing learning communities, such as those discussed in this book, where teachers have the opportunity to critique ideologies imposed on them and create knowledge from their own educational practice.

A hegemonic system that affirms one group as having dominance over all others (Apple 1996; McLaren 2003), and that confirms the status of academics as the legitimate knowledge creators, is unlikely to acknowledge the significance of personal knowledge, which for Polanyi (1958) formed an essential component in the construction of knowledge. Polanyi suggests that personal knowledge is often present at a tacit level, for example when the knower is unable to articulate explicitly the concepts that are known implicitly. He emphasizes his belief that such knowledge is valuable and indicative of the knower's commitment to understanding and interpreting their experiences: 'Into every act of knowing there enters a tacit and passionate contribution of the person knowing what is being known and this coefficient is no mere imperfection, but a necessary component of all knowledge' (ibid.: 312). Indigenous knowledge, which derives from a group's culture and social practices, is similarly disregarded by theorists who enjoy the status of knowledge creators under the traditional hierarchical system. Minority ethnic groups frequently suffer oppression and marginalization through having their personal knowledge ignored and discounted as potentially valid knowledge. Consequently, they feel that their culture is devalued and that they are perceived as having no worthwhile contribution to make to the development of knowledge in the dominant community in which they live and work. Arguing for a more democratic concept of knowledge, Hall (2016: 17) says such an approach 'recognises, values and supports the recovery and deepening of indigenous ways of knowing'. However, the education system can have a devastating influence on this situation, as May (1999: 1) explains, 'Not surprisingly, education – as a key institution of the (colonising) nation-state – has played a central part in the subjugation of indigenous languages and cultures and the related assimilation of indigenous peoples into the dominant or "common" language and culture of the nation-state.'

It would appear, then, that it is not in the interests of all members of society to privilege one group's knowledge over other ways of knowing, or to be dismissive of the knowledge contribution of minority groups. It is imperative, therefore, that academics are no longer regarded as the sole producers of knowledge, but that practitioners too are recognized as having a significant role to play in creating forms of knowledge that exemplify the practice of values of social justice, inclusion and democracy. The teachers who participated in the learning community outlined in Chapter 3 used a values-based approach in researching their practice and developing new knowledge about their practice. Similarly, in writing up my research for my PhD thesis (Sullivan 2006), I, as a practising teacher, outlined the relevance of my educational values, both at the level of theory and at the level of practice, to my efforts to gain equal rights to educational provision for a minority ethnic group. I believe that it is insufficient to identify and articulate one's values at a theoretical level: they need also to be realized and evident in one's living practice, thus establishing a firm link between abstract theory and concrete practice, which can be a positive outcome of teachers' participation in learning communities, as we demonstrate throughout this book.

# Reasons for traditional theory–practice dichotomy

I contend that the division between theory and practice is an artificial construct that benefits neither side, exalting the role of the theorist even as it diminishes the role of the practitioner. I suggest that the division may have developed from a narrow view of knowledge that portrays it as occurring only at the level of theory. This view discounts the possibility of practitioners creating their own theories of practice, and ensures that knowledge creation remains the preserve of academic theorists. Clarke (1994: 10) critiques the reductionist role that is often ascribed to teachers: 'I believe that the profession continues to cast teachers as implementers of dicta rather than as agents in the process of theory construction, curriculum planning and policy development.' Clarke (ibid.) is also critical of societal and professional tendencies to separate theory from practice, which, he feels, creates a disabling atmosphere for teachers and an unhealthy climate for education in general. It is worth noting that it is not only teachers who are disempowered through the traditional approach to knowledge creation: students can also feel powerless and alienated from the learning process if they are constantly perceived as receivers, rather than as able creators, of knowledge, as Elliott (2000: 182) indicates: 'What schools cannot do, in a traditional view of knowledge, is to bestow recognition and status on pupils for exercising autonomy within the learning process, since this view regards knowledge as static and passively acquired on the basis of authority rather than dynamic and actively constructed through inquiry'. The epistemological framework of the learning community, described in Chapter 3, contrasts sharply with the traditional view of knowledge as outlined above. Participating teachers were active agents to the extent that they chose their area of research, planned and carried out their proposed actions and articulated their findings: more importantly, they identified their new learning from the process and formulated it as a new theory of their practice. One teacher explained the change that occurred in her thinking from a powerless to a powerful stance: 'I seek expert/academic knowledge to apply sound principles to specific situations, but improvement lies within my understanding of the situation' (Feedback I, June 2011).

Another reason that academics might wish to maintain the traditional division between theory and practice is to do with the issue of power, and its effects on epistemological discourse. Foucault (1980b: 119) describes the symbiotic relationship that exists between knowledge and power, and says of the concept of power that 'it doesn't only weigh on us as a force that says no, but that it traverses and produces things, it induces pleasure, forms knowledge, produces discourse'. This understanding of power suggests that there is interdependence between it and the concept of knowledge. McLaren and da Silva (1993: 72) are also convinced that there is a strong connection between knowledge and relations of power: 'Knowledge is always indexical to the context of the knower and the known. In other words, knowledge is always implicated in relations of power and power is distributed laterally and historically, which is to say unequally among groups differentiated by race/ethnicity, gender and class.' It could be assumed, then, that those producing the knowledge are de facto the powerholders in society. It is hardly surprising, therefore, that academics would be slow to abandon their traditional role as the knowledge creators, as this would deprive them of their positions of power and leave them, in their view and perhaps to their consternation, on par with practitioners. They could perceive this situation as a diminishing of their status in the education hierarchy rather than seeing it as an opportunity for equalizing the relationship between academic and practitioner, and for engaging in robust and collaborative partnerships with classroom teachers. The learning community outlined in Chapter 3 was underpinned by equality of participation, with all teachers having equal opportunity to give voice to their opinions, and so power relations were not an issue during the process, as teachers willingly and generously shared ideas and expertise with one another. One participant acknowledged the value of sharing ideas with others: 'I bounce ideas off others more often ... At times, someone outside can help me see a situation from another angle' (Feedback E, June 2011).

# Reflective opportunity

What is your opinion of the traditional view that teachers are not capable of developing knowledge about their practice?

Why might academic theorists want to hold on to their role as the sole knowledge creators?

Do you agree with Schön that the problems in the swampy lowlands, that is, at the level of practice, are of the greatest human concern? Why?

# Various efforts aimed at reconciling the theory–practice divide

Various efforts have been made to break through the glass ceiling that seeks to separate theory from practice, and these have met with varying degrees of success. Action researchers have been particularly to the fore in attempting to dissolve the boundaries that have been erected and maintained frequently between theorists and practitioners. Those undertaking action research on their practice are well-positioned to engage in the task of trying to reconcile theory and practice because an action research approach is grounded in the principle that teachers are not only capable of researching their own practice, but also of developing a new theory of practice as they seek to bring about improvement in their classroom situations. Ghaye and Ghaye (1998: 69) maintain that 'action research is not only about learning: it is about knowledge production and about a commitment to improve practice'. Fitzallen and Brown (2016: 7) regard action research as an essential undertaking for teachers: 'The notion of embedding action research into the practice of teaching is increasingly becoming an expectation as teachers respond to the professionalization of teaching agenda.'

In contrast to the traditional view that seeks to maintain the theory–practice divide, and in agreement with many educational researchers worldwide

(Cochran-Smith and Lytle 2009a; Elliott 1998; Ghaye and Ghaye 1998; Kincheloe 2003; McLaren 2015; McNiff 2010; Stenhouse 1975; Whitehead 2015; Zeichner 2015), I subscribe to the idea that practitioners are eminently capable of creating knowledge, and therefore of developing their own theories from their practice (McDonagh et al. 2012; Sullivan et al. 2016). This approach contributes to a life-enhancing and productive role for practitioners that could position them in a more equitable relationship with academics. There are benefits for theorists also: they could experience an increase in their knowledge, and in the process, achieve the promotion of values of equality and social justice, through acknowledging the theory-developing capabilities of practitioners, and recognizing that there are other legitimate forms of knowledge besides academic knowledge.

Throughout the 1960s and 1970s, Stenhouse (1975) promoted the idea of teachers researching their practice as part of his Humanities Curriculum Project that was undertaken in secondary schools in the UK. He suggested that curriculum reform could be achieved through research-based practice, where teachers reflected on their actions and engaged in discussions around their practice. In a similar process, Elliot (1998) introduced the Ford Project, which supported the idea that educational change can occur through teachers engaging in research on their practice. He believed that free and open critical discourse could empower teachers to resist traditional structures of domination that characterized education systems. The Ford Project was undertaken with both primary and secondary teachers during the 1970s. The two initiatives mentioned here operated out of a view of teachers as competent researchers, capable of undertaking research on their practice and of developing a new theory from their practice, thus in effect combining theory and practice and minimizing any element of divisiveness between them.

Many other educational researchers have wholeheartedly supported the idea of teachers researching their classroom practice. Whitehead (1989; 1993; 2000; 2013; 2015) developed the idea that teachers can improve their practice through identifying their values and, as they try to live to those values, create living educational theories of their practice. McNiff (1993; 2010; 2013) suggested that teachers could engage in continuing cycles of action and reflection with the aim of improving their practice, and in the process develop new theories of practice. Cochran-Smith and Lytle (1999; 2009a) promoted the idea of teachers as researchers who can improve teaching and learning through carrying out enquiries into their practice and who are capable of generating theories that are grounded in their classroom practice. O'Hanlon (2002: 117) concurs with the view that educational theories can be developed by practitioners researching their practices: 'Theory is not produced by a group of "intellectuals" or experts who claim the right to generate valid knowledge. In educational research a wide range of techniques, methods and procedures are used, which allows researchers to define their own forms of valid knowledge, and present them as educational theories.' McLaren (2015: 28) discounts the possibility that theory and practice can exist as separate entities, saying that they are 'intrinsically linked in a dialectical unity'. He elaborates on this idea by stating that 'we treat theory as a form of practice and practice as a form of theory. In this way the production of knowledge can never be separated from praxis' (ibid.: 338). This is an apt depiction of the form of practical theory developed by the participants in the learning communities that we outline in this book.

In our learning community, where we cooperated and collaborated as we undertook our research for our PhD studies, which Máirín described in Chapter 1, we each developed theories from our individual practices in the manner suggested by the theorists cited above. In the following extract from Mary's PhD thesis, she outlines how this process emerged for her:

In relation to practice, I indicate how my living theory of the practice of freedom as a form of caring justice values the capacity of children for independence of mind and critical engagement, as well as their entitlement to opportunities to exercise this capacity in school. My living theory therefore has potential significance for other practitioners. I offer my living theory to other practitioners through this account as well as through making my work public in several other ways (at education conferences; through professional development in-service provision and workshops for teachers; through the publication of papers; and through communication with other researchers). In all cases I invite others to see if my work has relevance for them. I do not prescribe: I respect each practitioner's right to think for themselves.

In the domain of educational theory I demonstrate the significance of my living theory of the practice of freedom as commensurable with my values of justice and care and I explain how my theory builds on and differs from traditional propositional theories of care, freedom and justice in the literatures as I engage with these literatures in a critical way. (Roche 2007: 9–10)

Mary has articulated the importance of a critical stance and of critical self-reflection in developing a capacity to interrogate traditional beliefs and practices, such as the separation of theory and practice. Critical pedagogy, then, may provide the space for questioning some of these long-held views and perhaps for overturning them. McLaren (2015: 385) suggests that critical pedagogy 'gives us critical distance in examining our own epistemological and ontological formation'.

# The influence of critical pedagogy

Critical pedagogy is a discipline that allows for a broader interpretation of teaching and learning than the mere transmission of information. It encourages teachers and students to challenge ideologies and practices that perpetuate the dominant views, and to create their own knowledge through engaging in discourse and critical reflection. According to McLaren (2015: 32), critical pedagogy is about 'the hard work of building community alliances, of challenging school policy, of providing teachers with alternative and oppositional teaching materials'. He also suggests that there is a political dimension to critical pedagogy, which he describes as 'an anti-capitalist, anti-imperialist, anti-racist, anti-sexist and pro-democratic and emancipatory struggle' (ibid.: 27). Freire (2013: 124) was convinced of the power of dialogue in creating critical attitudes in the field of education in the following quotation, in which he refers to the participants in the dialogue as 'Subjects': 'Education is communication and dialogue. It is not the transference of knowledge, but the encounter of Subjects in dialogue in search of the significance of the object of knowing and thinking.'

McLaren (1999) believes that the ability of teachers to become critically self-reflective is intimately linked to the possibility of eschewing the tyranny of imposed theory developed by elite academics, thus paving the way for teachers to develop their individual epistemologies of practice. In his depiction of teachers as researchers, Kincheloe (2003) envisages this role as leading to the empowerment of teachers through providing them with skills and resources that enable them to reflect on their educational practice. He argues that 'research is an act which engages teachers in the dynamics of the educational process, as it brings to consciousness the creative tensions between social and educational theory and classroom practice' (ibid.: 40). As I engaged in classroom research for my PhD, and in the process developed a theory of my practice, I was influenced by the life-affirming and emancipatory views of the educational theorists quoted above as I demonstrated how my critical stance and self-reflection on my practice enabled me to develop a theory of that practice:

> Through the adoption of a more critical stance in my work, I have emancipated my own thinking and, consequently, have been able to engage in a practice of pedagogic freedom that has benefited both me and my pupils. In documenting the process of my learning in this account of my research, I wished to show how I hold myself accountable for implementing improvements in my practice and for accomplishing a developmental transformation in my thinking. The development of my thinking, through

the process of engaging in cycles of self-reflection and action, enabled me to theorise my practice. My embodied values of social justice and equality ensured that these principles underpinned the emerging living theories, as well as providing the conceptual frameworks for my research. (Sullivan 2006: 299)

We found that an effective way of resolving the issue of the theory–practice divide was to encourage teachers to undertake self-study action research projects that could provide them with the skills, the opportunities and the expertise required to demonstrate their capacity as knowledge creators in their educational practice. As they experience autonomy and self-efficacy, they can articulate their emergent theories of their enhanced practice, as was achieved by the teachers who participated in the learning community described in Chapter 3. One teacher articulated her new learning from her research as follows: 'I think that the most significant learning I got from this project is understanding what I am doing more thoroughly and understanding that I can improve it' (Feedback G, June 2011).

## Bridging the gap between academic and practitioner knowledge

Part of the rationale underpinning the division that has existed between academic and practitioner knowledge may relate to the particular form of knowledge produced by both parties. Academic knowledge usually stems from a positivist approach that seeks to be scientifically objective and aims for certainty and finality (McNiff 2015). It does not allow space for the personal perspective of the academic researcher, nor is it overly concerned with issues such as social justice, inclusion or democracy. Academic knowledge is often propositional in tone, generalizable and replicable in other situations if instructions are followed meticulously. The creation of practitioner knowledge, on the other hand, may be personal and subjective, emanating from within the teacher's own practice. It often operates out of a value-laden paradigm and adheres to strict ethical guidelines. Practitioner knowledge takes account of each teacher's specific context and circumstances, and so the findings can never be reproduced exactly in another teacher's particular classroom situation. Nevertheless, the creation of practitioner knowledge can be a powerful tool in facilitating the efforts of teachers to improve the quality of teaching and learning in their educational practice. Caitriona has indicated in her PhD thesis how she achieved an improvement in her own learning and in the learning of her students, thus creating new knowledge, as she carried out her research in a learning community that comprised herself and her students:

> In this chapter I am showing the formation of collaborative partnerships in education, where my children and I worked in an atmosphere of mutual respect; learning from and about each other while endeavouring to overcome obstacles within school structures in terms of pedagogy, curriculum and assessment. The changes that have occurred in my practice are not only practical actions but also reflect changes in my thinking. These changes in my thinking are related to my own new learning, which can be seen as in relationship with pupils' learning. The influence of their learning on my learning has convinced me that all individuals, given the opportunity, can make important contributions to new understandings of teaching and learning. The validity of my claim that these changes in my own practice influenced the changes in the children's practice was tested at several levels – in the classroom, in conference presentations and research seminars. (McDonagh 2007: 170)

It might seem as though the gap between the two forms of knowledge, academic and practitioner, could prove difficult if not impossible to bridge. However, as I have mentioned earlier in this chapter, and as Caitriona's extract above exemplifies, action research, carried out in a learning community, can provide the hybrid space that is capable of accommodating both epistemological positions, creating an opportunity for teachers to carry out research on their own practice and to develop new knowledge in the process. In his writing about efforts to improve the quality of school and college partnerships, Zeichner (2010: 89) proposes a similar solution when, in relation to teacher education, he argues that there is a need for a third space to ensure more inclusive and democratic ways of working: 'This work in creating hybrid spaces in teacher education where academic and practitioner knowledge and knowledge that exists in communities come together in new less hierarchical ways in the service of teacher learning represents a paradigm shift in the epistemology of teacher education programs.' MacLure (1996: 283) makes the point that action research seems to be concerned with transcending oppositions 'either by reversing the poles of the old dichotomies, so that practice gets privileged over theory, the practitioner over the researcher – or by seeking reconciliations, in which the interests of those who previously lived antagonistically on opposite sides of the boundary, will find a new space in which their differences can be resolved or dissolved'. I suggest that the latter option is preferable, from a standpoint of social justice and equality, which are the ontological values that frame my educational practice.

Action researchers reflect on their practice as they seek to improve it, identify their educational values, develop an action plan, monitor the plan as it is being implemented, keep a reflective journal as a record of changes made or improvements achieved, articulate their findings and produce a report of their findings, including their own learning from the process (McDonagh et al. 2012). Action research is a rigorous undertaking in which teachers try to live to their espoused values in their classroom practice. Throughout the process, the focus is on the self, as teachers ask 'How can I improve my practice?' (Sullivan et al. 2016; Whitehead and McNiff 2006). Their journey is a personal and continuous odyssey of enquiry into their practice as they seek to bring about improvement in it, and their critical self-reflection leads to new knowledge of that practice. The new knowledge thus created by educational practitioners can be expressed as a theory of practice when teachers provide robust evidence of their findings and when the evidence can be corroborated and validated by others, whether colleagues, students or parents. In my PhD thesis, I outlined the personal and professional enhancement that I experienced through carrying out my action research:

> The process of engaging in my research resulted in an enhancement in my personal and professional development. I suggest that such an outcome is consistent with a self-study practitioner research methodology (McNiff and Whitehead 2005), and therefore I propose to outline how an increase in self-knowledge and self-awareness resulted from my research, and thus contributed to the significance of the research at a personal level. Hamilton and Pinnegar (1998) consider a study of the self to be an important aspect of the research process. I suggest, then, that the process of developing living theories from my practice was linked to the process of my self-development, and that both processes were aspects of my research. The process of my self-development occurred through my critical reflection on my educational practice and through the subsequent explanations of my practice that I offer in this thesis, and that could be interpreted as explanations of a self, in terms of Spivak's (1988) understanding of this phenomenon. (Sullivan 2006: 272)

The idea of teachers as researchers, eminently capable of undertaking research on their own practice and developing theory in the process, is often met with resistance from policymakers, who perceive the task of teachers as being confined to the effective and efficient delivery of the prescribed curriculum. This definition of the role of teachers portrays them as technicians or implementers of others' ideas, whereas it might be more beneficial to both themselves and their students to allow them more autonomy in relation to curriculum and pedagogy. Haggerty (2004) bemoans the fact that teachers are pressured to teach as they are told, rather than encouraged to learn to teach differently and better, and to form more effective relationships with their students. It was the idea of teaching as conforming to the norms laid down by the gatekeepers that prompted hooks (1994: 4) to elucidate 'the difference between education as the practice of freedom and education that merely strives to reinforce domination'. Kincheloe (2003) promotes the idea of teachers as researchers as a means of developing the critical capacity of teachers so that they can create their own knowledge and be better placed to resist the imposition of top-down knowledge by dominant policymakers. Undertaking their research in cooperation and collaboration with colleagues has the potential to provide teachers with the impetus to reflect critically on their situation, and with the support needed to implement changes in their practice. In the extract below from her PhD thesis, Máirín shows how she engaged in different and innovative approaches that resulted in collaborative environmental projects in which communication was effected through the use of technology:

> I am claiming that I am developing an epistemology of practice that is grounded in dialogical, holistic and inclusional ways of knowing. I am experiencing this for myself as I theorise my practice. I perceive the interconnectedness of people and their environment as a locus that can enhance learning and I believe that people can develop their own learning potential and generate their own personal ways of knowing (Polanyi 1958). I believe that technology can enrich such interconnectedness and creativity. I can see that this new epistemology is significant not only for my own learning, but for others also. (Glenn 2006: 255)

It would seem, then, that teachers researching their own practice can articulate their personal knowledge and develop their theories of practice, and that this can be achieved through engaging in collaborative projects while participating in learning communities, as we demonstrate throughout this book.

# Reflective opportunity

What benefits might you gain through undertaking research on your own practice?

How might dialogue, as suggested by Freire, and critical self-reflection, as suggested by McLaren, result in a situation of empowerment for you?

What characteristics of action research might make it a suitable approach for you in researching your own practice?

# The role of learning communities in combining theory and practice

I now wish to explore the idea that learning communities can provide the conditions necessary to achieve a unity of theory and practice. Learning communities afford teachers the opportunity to cooperate and collaborate with colleagues in a partnership of equals. One of the main characteristics of a learning community is that it offers a space for members to engage in professional conversations, as outlined in earlier chapters. Such conversations are invaluable for teachers who wish to engage in a process of ongoing professional development. Morehouse (1991) suggests that conversation is the process that brings an idea, a feeling or an impression into the space between speaker and audience, and is convinced of its potency in ensuring that ideas are shared with the community. Discussing their ideas with others can help clarify, and expand on, the embryonic, individual and personal thoughts of teachers. As a result of their participation in such discussions, teachers can experience the articulation of their emergent ideas in the public domain, as well as an increase in their knowledge around the issues concerned. Hiebert et al. (2002: 13) refer to the benefits for teachers of opening up their practice to public scrutiny: 'Teachers would need to change their view that teaching is a personal and private activity and adopt the more risky but rewarding view that teaching is a professional activity that can be continuously improved if it is made public and examined openly.' Sharing ideas and engaging in dialogue around them with others in a participative and equitable forum can, as Morehouse (1991: 105) points out, 'create a community out of individuals'.

The initial conversations that take place in learning communities may be practice-based and practice-focused, as teachers outline concerns from their own classroom situations. As the communities make progress, and as teachers try out in their practice ideas gleaned from other participants, they may evolve into communities of enquiry, where teachers undertake research projects as they monitor the implementation of the new ideas in their individual situations. The critical reflection that this process requires could create a questioning mindset and a propensity towards engaging in ongoing practitioner research, reminiscent of Cochran-Smith and Lytle's (2009a) inquiry as stance, for the individuals involved. Researching their own practice can lead to teachers developing new knowledge about their practice, as we have seen in Chapter 3, and this new knowledge can be articulated as a theory of their practice. Theory and practice are combined in this process, and can be accommodated adequately and effectively under the rubric of learning communities.

Another characteristic of successful learning communities is that ideally they would be underpinned by principles of inclusion and social justice to ensure that all participants can partake and contribute on an equal basis. Inclusion makes for a more democratic, just and life-affirming approach that values all individuals and their contributions to the various discourses that take place. Having an inclusive outlook may help to avoid some of the pitfalls that can occur when discussions are taking place; for example, when there are divergent viewpoints, instead of having to opt for one or the other, participants may adopt an inclusive stance to accommodate both views. In such instances, they would be choosing a Platonic approach of 'both/and' rather than an Aristotelian one of 'either/or'. An inclusive framework would also allow participants in learning communities to unite elements of theory and practice in their collaborative endeavours.

# Reflective opportunity

Outline some ways in which professional conversations might be helpful to you as a participant in a learning community.
How might a learning community help to reconcile theory and practice?
What in your opinion are the benefits of an inclusive approach in a learning community?

# Learning communities as models for classroom interactions

Teachers who participate in learning communities may be inspired to use their experience as a framework for their classroom interactions with their students. The characteristics that contribute to successful learning communities for teachers would be equally valid as guiding principles for the practice of teaching and learning in schools. Teachers who have engaged in critical discourse with colleagues, and who value the opportunity for open and stimulating discussion, will often realize the significance of replicating these practices in their classrooms. Creating the conditions for students to participate in dialogue with their peers will encourage them to take ownership of their own learning and will contribute considerably to the honing of their critical thinking skills (Roche 2015). Bornstein (1991: 159) suggests that genuine dialogue, debate and conversation in the classroom should be framed by the following characteristics: 'Allowing students, within certain rules, to express themselves and give their opinions, ideas and points of view; facilitating and promoting the exchange of ideas and opinions, allowing interaction not only between the teacher and the students, but also, and more importantly, among students themselves.' These characteristics would help to create a more equitable relationship between teacher and students, and would have the potential to generate strong and robust pedagogic partnerships.

Participants in learning communities operate in an atmosphere of care, trust, integrity and respect for one another. These values could be seen as core qualities of a successful learning community and also as essential for successful classroom relationships. The Teaching Council of Ireland (2012b; 2016) promotes these as key professional values for all teachers. These values underpin 'the standards of teaching, knowledge, skill, competence, and conduct' (Teaching Council of Ireland 2016: 8). When relationships are based on such values, they are likely to promote the practice of social justice and equality. As we develop an understanding of learning communities in classrooms we look to Noddings (1992) who viewed the achievement of an ethic of care in schools as a challenge for teachers. She argues that education should be organized around the theme of care as an all-embracing value. Apple and Beane (1999: 13) argue for a wider interpretation of care as a characteristic of democratic schools, stating that 'those involved with democracy care deeply about young people, but they also understand that such caring requires them to stand firm against racism, injustice, centralized power, poverty and other gross inequities in school and society'. As conveners of learning communities, and as teachers in classrooms, we realize that perhaps the best way to promote a culture of caring is for us to model it in our relationships with others. As Noddings (1992: 22) says, 'we do not tell our students to care; we show them how to care by creating caring relations with them'.

Some schools focus almost exclusively on academic achievement, to the detriment of the emotional development of their students. Hargreaves (2003: 45) is convinced that teaching is not just a cognitive and intellectual activity, but also a social and emotional one: 'Good teachers fully understand that successful teaching and learning occur when teachers have caring relationships with their pupils and when their pupils are emotionally engaged with their learning.' The capacity of teachers to view their students as fellow human beings, rather than depicting them as 'The Other', could contribute to a more caring, fulfilling and life-enhancing experience of education for all. The ability of teachers to perceive themselves as co-learners with their students could create genuine and successful learning communities. hooks (1994: 153) describes how, at the start of each semester, she felt an onus 'to establish that our purpose is to be, for however brief a time, a community of learners together. It positions me as a learner.' In such a scenario, the pedagogic relationship would then be based on what Buber (1958) defines as 'I–Thou', rather than 'I–it', relationships: the former encapsulates positive elements such as equality, mutual respect, reciprocity and subjectivity, while the latter has inklings of unequal power relations, impersonal attitudes, indifference and objectivity.

# Reflective opportunity

What benefits can students gain through participation in learning communities?

Why is it important to have an ethic of care in schools?

What, according to Buber, is the difference between an 'I–Thou' and an 'I–it' relationship?

# To conclude

In this chapter, I examined the complexities of the traditional categorization of theory and practice as two separate entities, each occupying its own domain in the research hierarchy. I outlined the historic reasons for the rift between academic and practitioner, and explained why these reasons may not be valid. I recounted the various efforts that have been made to reconcile the differences that separated the two concepts, including the role of critical pedagogy in this regard. The distinction between academic knowledge and practitioner knowledge has been discussed, and the idea of engaging in self-study action research as a means of uniting the two forms of knowledge has been mooted. Examples from the authors' research have been provided to illustrate and confirm this possibility. I explored the prospect of learning communities becoming sites for the unification of theory and practice. Finally, I believe that I have presented a compelling rationale for my suggestion that the principles and practices governing the operation of learning communities could be applied usefully and beneficially to the pedagogic relationships in classroom practice.

# 5

# Professional Conversations as Integral to Self-Study Action Research for CPD

## *Mary Roche*

## Introduction

Three friends and I went out together recently. Two were teachers like myself, and one works in a business environment. When she heard who else was coming along she groaned, 'I'll have to listen to you teachers talking shop all night!' She has grounds for this assumption: when teachers get together it does not take much to get them discussing their practice. They frequently get straight into the heart of issues to do with social justice and care, although they may not have articulated these particular educational values. Over my teaching career I have attended a wide variety of CPD events. Like many teachers, I sometimes found these to be helpful. However, I often found the informal conversations over coffee to be more professionally enlightening. Informal chat quickly evolves into more in-depth conversation, because teachers have the wisdom of educational theory combined with the experience of daily practice, as we saw in Chapter 3. Teachers generally have a strong sense of equity and are anxious about meeting their students' needs. Having wrestled with complex classroom issues, they often have practical solutions to a diverse range of pedagogic and classroom management problems. What busy teachers and their school heads rarely have, perhaps, are sufficient opportunities during school time to share this knowledge with others in a structured way. They grab moments at lunchbreaks, during shared supervision duties or in hasty exchanges on corridors. And yet Seashore et al. (2003) state:

> The hypothesis is that what teachers do together outside of the classroom can be as important as what they do inside in affecting school restructuring, teachers' professional development, and student learning. (Seashore et al. 2003: 3)

None of this is new: over twenty years ago Eraut (1994) emphasized that professionals continually learn as they carry out their work, but he also made the point that unless specific time is set aside to deliberate and reflect, learning may not be incorporated into any general theory of practice.

In this chapter I explore:

- how the provision of spaces for professional conversations can lead to reflective, self-evaluative and emancipatory practice

- how a self-evaluative and emancipatory learning community developed

- the transformative potential of professional conversations

- use of online CPD courses as authentic spaces for professional conversation.

## The provision of spaces for professional conversations can lead to reflective, self-evaluative and emancipatory practice

Teachers generally need very little encouragement to set up their own professional learning groups where expertise can be shared. As we saw in earlier chapters, teachers are professionals who can straddle the boundaries between theory and practice. They can go beyond mere technique, and discuss essential professional questions: their philosophy of teaching, their educational values and their identity and integrity as teachers. It is important, we authors feel, that the identification and articulation of educational values are the launching pad for professional development. This may take some time to implement because discussion of such issues, however fundamental they may be to professional development, can sometimes be seen as 'alien to academic culture' (Palmer 1997: 12). Palmer argues that if we want to grow as teachers we must 'do something alien to academic culture: we must talk to each other about our inner lives … risky stuff in a profession that fears the personal and seeks safety in the technical, the distant, the abstract'.

I will now describe one particular professional learning group in which I was involved. I worked with a group of teachers as we formed a vibrant learning community that, I believe, evolved into a transformative experience for all participants and their institutions, similar to what we saw in Chapter 4. As you will see in the case study below, one teacher's enquiry, supported by her colleagues in the learning community, had an educative influence in both her learning and our learning. This impacted on her teaching and in turn, had a profound significance for the life of one particular child.

## *The beginning: what we did*

My co-authors and I planned a programme primarily aimed at helping teachers develop a space for dialogue such as is outlined by Palmer above. The idea was that this would be a sustainable process insofar as these teachers could then go on to set up their own networks and encourage their colleagues and possibly other teachers to do likewise. Our aim was to explore if, and how, we could assist teachers in designing a sustainable form of CPD that would help them to identify and connect with their personal values and philosophy of teaching. We hoped also that the initiative would encourage them to form supportive professional relationships through professional conversation, action and reflection. As we saw earlier, we wanted to move away from the traditional forms of CPD to which many teachers have become accustomed, which are often underpinned by a deficit model of professional development that suggests that teachers rely on other 'experts' to fill the supposed gaps in their professional development (Clark 2001: 5). Clark (ibid.) argues that generally such forms of CPD are top-down, contextually insensitive and based on short-term solutions, or what Conway et al. (2009: 7) refer to as the 'one-shot, knowledge transfer model'. We wanted to encourage teachers to design a more authentic, contextually sensitive model that would acknowledge the idea that they are professionals who are capable of critical reflection on their practice so as to make judgements about it. We were convinced of this because, as you saw in earlier chapters, we had experienced this ourselves.

As we said in our report for the Teaching Council of Ireland (Glenn et al. 2012: 10), we drew on the notion of 'teacher as theorist' (Kadi-Hanifi 2010; Whitehead and McNiff 2006). The project was grounded in educational values and in the idea that teachers' professional development and learning could be offered as a form of support that would encourage the participants to develop their own educational theories from their practice, rather than just passively accepting others' knowledge. We designed the course so that the participants would be sustained by belonging to a learning community where knowledge and expertise would be shared through professional conversation. We feel that teaching, like knowledge and like life itself, is a continuous ever-evolving process of construction and reconstruction. Good teachers are always seeking ways of learning to teach better. As you will see, our group soon evolved into a professional learning community. Bolam et al. (2005: 223) suggest that a professional learning community is at heart a community of people 'sharing and critically evaluating their practice in an ongoing, reflective, collaborative, inclusive, learning-oriented and growth-promoting way'. It is not just about reflection however: the primary function of the professional learning community is acting on that learning so as to enhance the learning of all, or what Freire (1970) called praxis, that is, critical reflection along with morally informed action.

Our first organizing framework for this research project with teachers was located in the principles of self-study action research. The second was grounded in the principles of teachers participating in professional, authentic, learning conversations as outlined in the work of Clark (2001). We endorse Clark's view that:

> Our collective experiences put the lie to the cynical view that when teachers have the freedom to talk together, they waste time on superficial ... matters. On the contrary, the common ground that unites teachers ... are the mysteries of learning, teaching, and life in all its complex relationships. (Clark 2001: 172)

As you will see, the teachers we met were deeply reflective, and used this critical reflection to investigate their practice and provide answers to their professional concerns. I argue that these teachers all displayed the wholeheartedness, open-mindedness and intellectual responsibility of Dewey's (1933) reflective practitioner. Dewey identified these three key characteristics as being essential for reflection. The teachers also exhibited the criticality of what Hoyle (1975) calls the extended professional as he spoke about how some teachers do not remain at the level of technician but cross the boundaries between theory and practice. From the outset the teachers we met were committed to improvement of practice and engagement with the enquiry process. They enjoyed it. Many commented on how nourishing and energizing it was to meet and talk on a regular basis with like-minded professionals (Glenn et al. 2012). In a few moments we will examine what happened as we organized an information evening. But first let's take a little time out to reflect.

# Reflective opportunity

When was the last time you and a group of colleagues had a genuine professional conversation?

What was discussed? What did you contribute? What did you learn?

When was the last time you and colleagues discussed the values that underpin your practice?

# Developing a self-evaluative and emancipatory learning community

I will describe this in five developmental phases. The first occurred during the information meeting and developed at each meeting that followed. I will then use a case study of a specific teacher to explain the rest of the process.

## *Information night*

We began by advertising for teachers to engage in a course that would enable them to design their own CPD. I organized an information evening in the local education centre. A group of about thirty teachers from primary, post-primary and further education contexts were present at this initial meeting. It is interesting to note that while there are hundreds of teachers in the catchment area, only thirty or so responded. The reasons as to why people attend or ignore such courses/information nights would, in itself, merit further study. At the information meeting, I explained the principles of self-study action research and I described how it offered a viable alternative to current CPD delivery models. I outlined how I hoped that participants would explore ways of rejuvenating or celebrating their teaching and of redefining their professional learning. I described how they could gather the data and evidence necessary to enable them to construct and/or modify their theories of practice. This, I explained, could be done in their individual sites of practice and added that I hoped that they would embrace the notion of 'inquiry as stance' (Cochran-Smith and Lytle 2009b), and see their professional inquiry as a new way of being. I suggested that workshop-type meetings of two hours' duration would be held in the Education Centre once a month over a school year where teachers would be facilitated in identifying an area of practice in which they would like to improve, and then be supported as they sought ways of bringing about that improvement. I explained that there would be no fees and no accreditation, but that it would require critical reflection and a written account of the project. During and following each workshop, I explained, participants would be asked to reflect on their learning, to problematize it and to share their ideas. I also explained that I would be researching my role in the process for the Teaching Council of Ireland, and was given permission to write about it. This is what I wrote in my journal at that time:

> After I had outlined what would be involved, I gave some time to the teachers present to think about, and discuss, the values that they felt informed how they acted in their classrooms, and what they thought might be a possible area of their practice that might merit closer examination. They were invited to share these with the group. Some teachers found this easy: others struggled to articulate values and identify an area of concern. I reassured them that this was quite normal. Teachers are rarely asked to do such specific reflection after graduating from Initial Teacher Education institutions (unless they get involved in a postgraduate programme that is grounded in critical reflection) and such answers do not always arrive on demand. I provided some examples from case studies of work I had done with an MEd group in the local university. I showed how one small piece of action research can often have a significance far beyond the immediate classroom context. Teachers shared with me, and with each other, the fact that they had not been asked previously to identify their values or articulate their concerns. Some said they would need time to think about this. When I asked if articulating values would be a useful thing to do at a staff meeting, most shook their heads: reasons varied: 'we're just not that close'; 'our opinions don't matter, so why would our values? We usually just get dictats and directives from our principal'. One positive response was: 'it would make sense to do this, after all we have a school mission statement: this is like each of us making our own personal mission statement.' (Reflective Journal, October 2010)

We have written elsewhere (McDonagh et al. 2012; Roche 2015; Sullivan et al. 2016) about how values matter. They are the foundation and support, as well as the guiding path for our practice. Values are not static: they evolve as our knowledge evolves. They are a launch pad for our investigation into our practice. We authors cannot imagine beginning any research without first carrying out critical reflection on our values.

During the discussion that ensued at the information meeting, a primary teacher called Emily said, 'My biggest concern is that there are some pupils in my class (age ten to eleven years) that I find really difficult to teach.' Emily worked in a school that had almost a thousand pupils and had very little prior knowledge of the children in her class. I suggested she might try consulting with the pupils. She did so and related the ensuing suggestions at the first group meeting. Emily went on to become part of a core group that met monthly and her story will form the main case study of this chapter.

# Reflective opportunity

What values might you have articulated if you had been there?
What might you have identified as an area of professional concern?
What do you think you could do about it?
What might you have suggested to Emily that she should do?

## *The first meeting*

Following the information evening, several teachers signed up and were invited to come to the first group meeting about two weeks later. They were asked to come prepared to discuss a possible area of focus for their self-study. I had reflected on what I believed my role should be. As we saw in previous chapters, I felt that I should be a guide and resource. It was exciting for me to listen as each person presented their area of concern and observe as the combined years of teachers' theoretical and practical experience led to huge engagement with problems and a variety of solutions being offered. As people spoke, everyone listened – some took notes, and some interjected with ideas as they were struck by something someone said. Some offered suggestions as to where teachers might find literatures to support the conceptual frameworks of their various research areas. A few days later, one of the teachers contacted me. He said: 'I was so impressed with the format and the creation of this democratic space that two other teachers and I have decided to set up a similar learning group amongst the staff in our school.' This was exactly what my colleagues and I were hoping for: that the more formal meetings would be a model for the creation of similar professional learning spaces in participants' own contexts.

Now let's return to examine more closely one particular case study. There were professional conversations between the teachers in the group as well as between Emily and her pupils. With her permission, I have selected Emily's experience, and I will show how the different professional conversations that ensued led to significant learning for all of us in the group, and also had a profound influence in the learning of Emily's students.

### Case study: Emily's story

Having examined her values and reflected on her primary concern, Emily felt that she needed to focus on differentiation and establish for herself if she inadvertently allowed some children to dominate in her class. At that first meeting, she had articulated clearly her core values about freedom and care, and she had related how she felt that each student should be valued for who they were and that no student should be left behind. This had sparked an animated conversation in the group about how difficult it can be to try to live one's educational values fully in a system where, for example, large class sizes are the norm.

I was interested in the kind of suggestions made: I wonder could you try ...; Maybe if you ...; I had a similar problem and I ...; What about if you ...; We've been talking and we think that .... No one was prescriptive or overbearing. Despite the disparate age range and experience levels, the teachers were all tentative and supportive and collegial in their language. (Notes on first meeting, October 2010)

## Second meeting

At the next meeting Emily told us about some requests that the children had made in response to her dialogue with them about how she might help them learn better.

I have begun to observe the children more, with particular attention to the four children who were struggling. Following suggestions from the group, I decided to ask those children how I might best help them to learn. Their first request surprised me: they wished us to have regular class meetings where they could air their opinions. I agreed to monthly meetings. While I initially thought most of the class issues were to do with differentiation, it seemed from the children's feedback, that it was more to do with class organisation, so I have shifted my attention to fairness and equality in the class. This is also in line with what I have been reading. Again when I brought my account to the group meeting, there was lively discussion around ways of treating children with more equity. Several suggestions were made around the idea that the children might itemise further areas which they felt could be dealt with more fairly, and this time, they should offer solutions rather than wait for me to solve things for them. (Emily's Learning Journal, October 2010)

## Third meeting

At the next meeting it became obvious to me that the participants were quite confident about their own sense of identity. Not only were they effective teachers in their own contexts, but they now recognized that they had the agency that allowed them to begin to improve and change their own practices, as well as advise and assist Emily. This probably would not be evident in a 'normal' top-down CPD context. These teachers were shaping their own growth and, through professional conversation, were helping a colleague to do the same. Emily, in turn, was often in a position to offer advice to others who presented their problems to the group.

As the teachers shared ideas I noticed that there was equality and parity of esteem amongst them despite the varying degrees of age and experience. For example, when Emily spoke about needing to ensure equity, one teacher explained how teaching for equality can often lead to inequity because equality can rely on a one-size-fits-all mentality whereas teaching for equity can result in real equality. This was debated and discussed at a philosophical as well as at a personal level. One person referred to how teachers must focus on connecting with their students. Palmer (1997) speaks about the need for connecting with other teachers and revealing our vulnerabilities. I felt that this was exactly what these teachers were doing: they were revealing insecurities and fragilities but in return they were being supported and scaffolded in finding solutions to their pedagogical problems. However this was mainly because these problems affected learning. It was not merely a focus on how to teach better; the emphasis was on how to help children learn better.

## *Fourth meeting*

Emily continued to share her learning and again the teachers in the group offered more suggestions. Some also asked for clarification around the strategies Emily had acquired, and wanted to use some of them themselves. Each teacher also contributed their own evolving stories of how their self-study was progressing. There was rich discussion and sharing of advice and teaching approaches. It was real dialogue with communication of ideas, attentive listening, exploration and discovery.

Emily continued to bring her descriptions and explanations of what was taking place in her thinking and in her practice to each subsequent meeting of the group (as did each of the other participants). People commented, pondered, asked questions, provided additional ideas and Emily participated and took notes and qualified her statements and modified her ideas. It was a rich, engaging dialogue. I learned subsequently that these professional conversations continued after each meeting with several members of the group sharing conversations by email. Emily explained how, as a result of the continuing conversations with her pupils, her children were no longer resentful of some of the decisions she made, as they now understood the reasoning behind them. She wrote:

They are more engaged in the class. They are also becoming more independent in their learning. Now that they are comfortable with their new classmates, they are also more willing to ask for help, share ideas and knowledge and help each other. They know now when to ask for help and when to try harder themselves to figure something out. (Emily's Learning Journal, January 2011)

I began to realize that Emily's classroom conversations and experiences were mirroring what was also happening in our learning community. As the time went on I could see clearly how the provision of this space for professional conversations was leading to critically reflective, self-evaluative and emancipatory practice in all contexts. Up to this all seems to be positive: now we will examine a perceived setback that was encountered.

### A setback

The weeks and months went by. Each teacher in the group had achieved clarity and deeper understanding of their practice. One person, Anne, (not her real name) did not continue with the meetings. When she was articulating her concern around classroom management issues at an early meeting, another teacher with a strong personality told her that she just needed to 'get stricter at insisting on good behaviour'. At the time I was unaware that this comment caused Anne distress, but she later emailed me to say she felt I had not created a sufficiently safe atmosphere for the group. I felt really guilty and apologized profusely for my lack of awareness of her discomfort. I entreated her to attend the next meeting where I would do my best to restore her confidence in the process. She declined. It bothered me for a long time after the project ended, and still bothers me, that I was the reason why she did not persevere. From this experience I conclude that facilitators/conveners might benefit from some guidance on group dynamics and leadership.

## Reflective opportunity

If you were facilitating a group like this what would your response have been to Anne?
What should or could I have done differently?
Why might professional development in group leadership/dynamics be necessary?

## The transformative potential of professional conversations

At each meeting we became accustomed to Emily's quiet, matter-of-fact narratives of practice and each time we were agog at the democratic learning environment her pupils enjoyed. And then one evening she arrived downcast and despondent. She brought with her some samples of the classroom magazine that was one of her pupil-collaboration successes. She was downcast as she showed us how some pages were defaced by ugly scribbles and marks. She explained how one boy in particular was acting up and seeking to sabotage the hitherto-enjoyed process. She was baffled by his behaviour and sought advice. Teresa suddenly said: 'I don't know why I think this but ... could this child be grieving?' It transpired that she had personal experience of working with a bereaved child. Emily duly looked into the child's personal history and it was so: he had lost his father during the previous year. In a very large school it is easy for the facts of a child's life to be overlooked. Serendipitously, the following day I found a book about bereavement in children (McAuslan and Nicholson 2010). It was aimed at explaining to children how, after suffering the loss of a close relative, they will feel sad and lonely most of time. However, the book also explains to them that they sometimes might experience periods of happiness too. This can result in feelings of guilt or anger. Teresa had correctly deduced that perhaps Emily's pupil had begun to enjoy participating in the classroom magazine activity and perhaps, felt guilty about forgetting his dad for a while. Therefore unconsciously perhaps, he may have tried to destroy the magazine activity so as to be admonished and revert to feeling bad. Emily gave the book to the boy, who asked if he could take it home.

## *Transformation in the life of a vulnerable child*

Having a space for engaging in professional conversation as these teachers did, led to a significant episode in the life of this troubled child: Emily's pupil was in fifth class (age 10–11). His behaviour was rapidly deteriorating, and had this not been investigated by a caring teacher such as Emily, prompted by an experienced teacher like Teresa, the boy could have gone into his final primary school class labelled as troublesome. This label could easily follow him into post-primary and who knows what the outcome might have been for him. Had Emily not been supported by the group in reflecting on ways of differentiating in her class, had she not reflected critically on creating a safe and democratic learning environment for each of her pupils, a child's life chances could have been compromised. Emily's own professionalism was enhanced; her understanding of her educational values and her critical scrutiny of her practice, so as to live those values more fully, led her to a deeper understanding of what Palmer (1997) calls 'identity and integrity' which, he says, 'have as much to do with our shadows and limits, our wounds and fears, as with our strengths and potentials ... They are subtle dimensions of the complex, demanding and life-long process of self-discovery' (13).

# Reflective opportunity

What are your thoughts about the significance of the incident
described above?
Have you experienced any such critical learning moments?
What were they? How did they come about?

# Professional conversations and core professional qualities

From the case study above I believe that it can be seen that the teachers
who participated in our learning community, although very different in age
and experience, and situated in varying teaching contexts, matched the
profile of the 'extended professional', a term coined in the 1970s by Hoyle
as outlined by Evans (2008), who argues that 'the characteristics of the
model of extended professionality ... reflect: a much wider vision of what
education involves, valuing of the theory underpinning pedagogy, and the
adoption of a generally intellectual and rationally-based approach to the
job' (28). Individually the participants were critically reflective in that they
recognized that pedagogical problems rarely have one quick-fix solution.
They were willing to examine their practice through several lenses before
coming to any conclusions, much as Brookfield (1995) suggested. They were
prepared to try different approaches, monitor the action, reflect and discuss
their findings with others. These teachers demonstrated that they shared
the characteristics of Dewey's (1933) reflective practitioner, in that they were
open-minded, wholehearted and displayed intellectual responsibility (see also
Sullivan et al. 2016). Most were good listeners and were generally observant,
generous and empathetic towards each other. Many showed that they were
enquiry-oriented with strong intellectual curiosity. There was a sense of
collective wisdom, passion for learning, positivity, agency and self-efficacy
in the group. Most participants showed that they were comfortable with the
idea of searching for, identifying and articulating their educational values. To do
this they used written individual reflections as well as shared 'talk, narrative,
conversation and dialogue' (Clark 2001: 157). Clark (ibid.) believes that among
teacher groups these four different forms of teacher talk are important, and
that each has a specific purpose and quality of learning associated with it. Like
Emily, each participant brought narratives, anecdotes and reports of practice
to our meetings. These then engendered professional conversation, dialogue,
discussion and ordinary talk. For example, in our report we showed how one
participant commented: 'Often in the *telling* comes something previously not

articulated. It was fascinating to watch the others *speak* aloud their concerns and then speak their way into possible solutions to their own concerns. This is a powerful message to other teachers and researchers. The answers may come from within you or from the group' (Glenn et al. 2012: 20).

Another aspect of the particular traits of these professionals was their openness to the idea of development, change and transformation. In our report (Glenn et al. 2012), we spoke of how participants commented on how group discussion and sharing of ideas meant they were empowered to approach areas that were of personal professional concern. Many found the project to be life-changing and transformative. One teacher admitted that she was never very courageous at initiating change prior to doing this project. She described how she felt that talking her ideas through with like-minded, committed professionals in a safe environment provided her with a context for widening her knowledge and understanding, as the group teased out with her the various approaches and strategies she could use to solve her particular concern. Others said that in trying to help a colleague solve a thorny problem, they reached a new understanding of their own practice. Many others stated that they liked the fact that self-study was a grass-roots enquiry approach that addressed their individual needs. Each teacher generated their own opportunities for learning from their own situations. One teacher commented that she believed that this type of professional learning would be really appropriate for anyone interested in improving their teaching and understanding of teaching. Another teacher articulated it as each participant fine-tuning their research to their own specific needs (Glenn et al. 2012).

Over the duration of the project we authors shared our findings with each other. As we engaged in professional dialogue around our work we each saw how our learning was also exciting and transformative. We wrote in our report that we found the experience to be 'living, cumulative and developmental' (Glenn et al. 2012: 23). We stated too that we felt that as each teacher examined their own research topic, their exploration and findings added to the development of the whole group. We also developed new personal understandings about the significance of collaborative self-evaluation. For example, we stated in our report:

We saw how it allowed teachers to empower themselves to build on their professional strengths. We were entirely convinced of the viability of the project and the value of self-study action research as a way of researching and improving practice.... We saw how our own personal and professional strengths contributed to the learning for participants as we worked towards weaving a safe and collaborative environment for all. We noted how, in all cases, pupil learning was of paramount importance. (Glenn et al. 2012: 23)

This can be seen also in Bolam et al.'s (2005: iii) definition of an effective professional learning community: 'An effective professional learning community has the capacity to promote and sustain the learning of all professionals ... with the collective purpose of enhancing pupil learning'. Throughout the sessions, and in their evaluations, the participants expressed enthusiasm about their teaching lives and were very passionate about the project. In particular, they liked the opportunities for educational dialogue and nourishment that were provided by their participation in a learning community, at both the personal and professional level. None of this would have been possible however without the various 'extended professional' (Evans 2008) traits demonstrated by the participants, of critically and reflectively linking theory and practice, engagement in dialogue, and a strong commitment to authentic and relevant professional development.

I believe that the following extract demonstrates powerful evidence of the sustainability of action research. The events described took place in 2010/ 1. Having drafted this chapter I sent it to Emily (in August 2016), as I had promised. Her response shows the sustainability of her learning and how this CPD is still valid for her and for her pupils:

> I have to say I was in tears at your description of my pupils and at the reminder of all the work we did that year! I recently met a parent of a girl in that class.... She thanked me for the time the child received that year as it was 'the makings of her': until that year, a difficulty with English had gone unnoticed. Due to the work we did (in our learning community) this girl was 'heard' and the difficulty unmasked. She was an excellent student and because she was quiet, polite, hardworking etc., she was able to hide her shortcomings, but when she was given the forum to speak up and verbalise difficulties without fear of being laughed at, she admitted needing extra help and according to Mom 'thrived ever since'. I can honestly say I wouldn't have been able to help her in that way without my involvement in our learning community and how lovely, years later, to get feedback from her Mom. (Email from Emily, August 2016)

# Online CPD courses as professional conversation spaces

Along with our face-to-face courses we authors also provided several online courses. These courses were an effort to answer one of the questions that arose from the commissioned research we carried out for the Teaching Council of Ireland (Glenn et al. 2012): the difficulty of accessing CPD encountered by some teachers because of issues such as geographical location or competing family commitments. We structured our online courses around five main modules: critical reflection; principles of action research; thinking critically and examining one's values; taking action, gathering data and evidence; significance of action research. Almost 200 teachers participated in our online summer courses and they were scattered throughout the country.

## Generating discussion and critical engagement in an online course

When we were designing the course we sought ways of engaging teachers in genuine professional dialogue and critical thinking. We wanted to stimulate the kind of interactive participant-to-participant and participant–facilitator model that worked so well in the face-to-face course. 'Student-to-instructor and student-to-student interactions are important elements in the design of a Web-based course ... because learners can experience a "sense of community", enjoy mutual interdependence, build a "sense of trust", and have shared goals and values' (Ya Ni 2013: 201). She also states that the social and communicative interactions are important. 'It is often through conversation, discourse, discussion, and debate among students and between instructors and students that a new concept is clarified, an old assumption is challenged, a skill is practised, an original idea is formed and encouraged, and ultimately, a learning objective is achieved' (ibid.: 201). She suggests that online discussions, through text only, are frequently structured, dense, permanent, limited and stark whereas face-to-face discussions are verbal and impermanent.

We agree with Ya Ni because, during the first iteration of our course, we noticed that there was a lack of critical engagement in the discussion forum. The participants seemed to be going through the motions of responding to direct questions rather than engaging in any real dialogue. With this in mind we decided to include a link to a prizewinning Japanese film *Children Full of Life* (2003). We hoped that watching the film, reflecting on it and sharing their responses would allow teachers an opportunity to dialogue together as they articulated their reactions to the film. In the film a male teacher of a fourth grade class (age 9–10) instructs his students to write their inner feelings in letters and read them aloud to the whole class. As they share their lives, the children begin to realize the importance of caring for each other.

## Reflective opportunity

Why not watch the film and note your own responses before continuing? Follow the link http://kobreguide.com/children_full_of_life/ or simply enter 'Children Full of Life' into your search engine.

My instructions to the course participants were as follows (note: you won't see this in your browser: this was on our course only): 'In the film we see a teacher trying to prepare his pupils for life – *his* way. The film has been awarded prizes and has been well received internationally. Underneath the video clip you will see responses to the film from different professionals. I'd be really interested in hearing what you all think of the film.' (In advance I had sent the link to the film to some professionals working in different educational contexts: a school counsellor, a child psychologist, a school librarian, a mature teacher and a young male teacher in order to get a variety of perspectives that might spark a discussion.)

The school counsellor did not like the film at all:

> I do not consider the approach to be conducive to positive empathy, it feels forced and contrived, and, while I like the reflective element of their behaviour recorded in their diaries, I think it is most unsafe to expose some children, who may be more vulnerable than others, to letting out their feelings to their peers. (Online Discussion Forum, 2013)

This response provoked a lively outcry from some course participants. Unsurprisingly, the film also generated an amazing variety of passionate responses from the participants:

- I found this video the most thought-provoking item I've viewed so far on this module! I was amazed though, at some of the very strong reactions of those who gave feedback, particularly the counsellor. I disagree with the counsellor: I've never been comfortable with the idea that you can't comfort an upset child in the way any caring parent or adult would, which is all he very publicly did.
- My impression was that he had his students best interests at heart, he did give his students moral guidance and got his students to begin to think critically on topics central to everyday life like bullying, punishment and death, and to paraphrase Noddings – to neglect critical thinking on topics central to everyday life is to make the word education virtually meaningless.
- I loved the fact that this film allows us to make links with the other critical questions we were asked to think about. For instance, I feel there is definitely a difference between schooling and education … The teacher in the Japanese film paid attention to the basic elements of schooling as well as to the bigger issues shown in the video.
- Yes I agree with N. I like the fact that the film gave us an opportunity to link theory and practice. I think the problem-posing approach is much better than the banking approach. (Online Discussion Forum, 2013)

The data carries on in a similar vein, with some responses more lengthy than others. The 'Japanese film' triggered by far the greatest debate during our summer course and it was mentioned again by some people in their final evaluations. It shows however, that there can be real engagement, and a definite effort to engage in critical thinking if suitable 'incentives' and prompts are provided. However, the respondents seemed to be speaking to us course leaders rather than to each other. We have to speculate as to whether they were genuinely interested in dialogue or merely commenting, so as to be seen to fulfil the requirements of the course.

In relation to the significance or otherwise of this online course, while we have no data to show that anyone's practice was transformed as a result of doing the course, the evaluations were generally very positive. For example:

- It focussed the inquiry onto myself and got me thinking of myself in the role of a learner. It has inspired me to create a more student-oriented learning environment. In September, I aim to have more discourse among the pupils and to be more of a risk-taker in my lessons. It has made me realize how I can become a more reflective and critically thinking teacher.
- I think the suggestions made throughout the course could be looked at by the whole staff and they need to see how valuable a collaborative, team approach is in enhancing the working of the school. I think that when teachers work together and discuss their ideas, reflections and evaluations, not only do they forge greater professional relations, but it allows planning to be done at a much more meaningful level. (Online Course Evaluations, 2013)

There was a realization of the worth of evaluating one's practice by keeping a research diary, of reflective practice in general, and of the need for collaborative practice and dialogue. Our subsequent online courses were organized around similar content and generated similar responses. Designing and facilitating the course provided us authors with a stimulating series of discussions around what should and should not be included. It afforded us opportunities to include material on critical pedagogy which, in our experience, is rare in teacher summer in-service, where content is frequently more to do with the technical aspects of pedagogy. It offered us new learning around course design and evaluation, and also challenged our varying degrees of technological prowess. Overall we felt that some participants certainly engaged at the level we had envisaged when we began the process. We recognize many of the disadvantages, such as how to evaluate whether responses were authentic or not. But this would most likely be the case in any kind of professional development course. The main disadvantage we perceived in the online model was to do with a diminished listener–speaker relationship because of the asynchronous nature of the course and because content was mainly in a printed format where the lack of personal encounter and the subsequent inability to read facial expression, tone of voice and body language limited the interaction. Unlike the face-to-face learning community meetings outlined earlier, where participants engaged in real professional dialogue about authentic concerns around their practice, the online course was largely based on propositional knowledge, in the form of videos and reading materials provided by us authors. Granted, the online participants were all thinking for themselves as they made their responses. However, the face-to-face course ran for most of a school year and required the teachers to carry out a piece of research in their own classrooms for which their own teaching was the focus. There was a more concrete transformative aspect to the face-to-face course that was enabled and developed through the quality of professional conversation and human engagement.

# To conclude

We have seen how the provision of spaces for professional conversations, in the form of a particular face-to-face learning community, led participants to realize some of their potential as reflective, self-evaluative and emancipatory practitioners. We also saw the sustainable and transformative potential of professional conversations for the participants and their students. Besides, it afforded us opportunities to reflect on our roles as conveners/facilitators. We are left with several questions. For example, we would like to explore if certain practitioners with particular professional traits are more attracted to processes of enquiry such as self-study action research, and more likely to participate in learning communities and what, if any, is the link between this and Evans's (2008) and Hoyle's (1975) characterization of the extended professional – a critically reflective professional committed to theory and practice and who engages in relevant and challenging professional development with a genuine view to improving as a professional.

In relation to online CPD courses, we feel that we need to carry out further study on whether such courses can provide an authentic space for professional conversations, first of all because that was not our original rationale in designing the courses, and second because the technology has improved immensely even in the intervening few years. For example, Skype-type environments, where people can hear and see each other and observe reactions and body language, would likely improve the quality of the interaction. While these aren't perfect, they are possibly closer to capturing the quality of synchronous face-to-face interaction. We intend to explore how we can develop a combination of face-to-face and online interactions in our future research. As Máirín mentioned in Chapter 1, we have begun this process with our Network of Educational Action Research Ireland (NEARI).

# 6

# Initial Teacher Education and School–College Partnerships: The Potential Role of Self-Study Action Research

*Mary Roche*

## Introduction

Student teachers in most initial teacher education contexts are obliged to engage in a school placement process, sometimes referred to as 'a practicum'. According to Bezzina et al. (2006: 748), becoming a teacher requires far more than acquiring a relevant body of knowledge and skills. They suggest that the process is transformative in nature because it involves developing one's own personal and professional identity. They also argue that there is a need for teacher educators to work closely with teachers in schools in a dialogic partnership:

> The scenario we want is one which encourages, develops, nurtures and sustains professional dialogue which enhances the teaching and learning experience of all participants which now no longer involve student, class and university tutor only, but is extended further to include mentor and cooperating teacher. (Bezzina et al. 2006: 750)

For all student teachers, the school placement experience represents the first step on the teaching continuum. However, like Kalmbach Phillips and

Carr (2010), we authors argue that teachers, at all stages of the professional continuum, are always in the act of becoming, and we have seen at first-hand how self-study action research can be a powerful tool for assisting this process. By critically examining our teaching practice with a view to improving and becoming, we strive to be better at what we do, irrespective of where on the continuum of teaching we are. The reason we want to be better is, of course, always to do with improving the educational experience for learners. Below, I will set out a case study for how the partnership might be reconceptualized. I outline how self-study action research, undertaken by a student teacher and supported by ITE staff and school placement tutor/supervisors, can have significant potential for all stakeholders, with a focus on enhancing pupil learning. I acknowledge that the model I propose is not without challenges, not least of which is the acceptance of the validity of self-study action research values, principles and practice.

In this chapter I explore:

- how a 'researcherly disposition' can be fostered at ITE level and developed it through the school–college partnership model

- a case study: a model of SSAR for establishing a researcherly disposition

- what is the potential significance of this approach for the school–college partnership

- what is the potential learning for participating student teachers and education lecturers.

# Fostering a 'researcherly disposition' at ITE level and developing it through the school–college partnership model

Before we examine the case study let's look briefly at *the idea of partnership, the background landscape of school placement, and some of the challenges involved.*

## *Partnership*

Partnership is a difficult concept to define. Much has been written about it. For example, in the introduction to their paper, Fancourt et al. (2015: 353) speak about the 'plethora of research' that has sought 'to describe, interpret and improve what are often called "school-university partnerships" '. Healey et al. (2014: 4) propose some approaches in which they suggest the development of 'partnership learning communities' that may help to guide and sustain practice. They state that 'engaging students and staff effectively as partners in learning and teaching is arguably one of the most important issues facing higher education in the 21st century' (ibid.: 12). They suggest that partnership in this context 'is framed as a process of student engagement, understood as staff and students learning and working together to foster engaged student learning and engaging learning and teaching enhancement. In this sense partnership is a relationship which all participants are actively engaged in and stand to gain from the process of learning and working together'(ibid.). Galvin et al. (2009: 9) define partnership as a working relationship characterized by a 'shared sense of purpose, mutual respect, and the willingness to negotiate ... a sharing of information, responsibility, skills, decision-making and accountability'. They identify some of the core attributes [of partnerships] 'which resonate across the literature. These include attention to power relations, respect, sharing of information, and finally empathetic practice' (ibid.). These core attributes echo the qualities of communities of practice outlined by Stoll et al. (2006). Conway et al. (2009) argue that research on the effective professional development of teachers highlights the importance of both acknowledging and utilizing the funds of knowledge that the various stakeholders bring to teacher education. They suggest that new learning identities are generally shaped by the participation structures offered to learners and suggest that the strategic building of learning partnerships between universities and schools is 'essential for generating a framework for new modes of professional engagement, participation, lifelong learning and for creating the kinds of structures that synergistically prepare teachers for active engagement in shaping the 21st century professional' (ibid.: 189).

## *The background landscape of school placement*

In Ireland the placement of student teachers in schools is largely a process of goodwill between individual host schools and the institution providing the ITE. According to the Teaching Council (2013: 8), 'host schools are encouraged to be communities of good professional practice and to engage of their own accord with ITE ... From 2014, all postgraduate programmes of initial teacher education must be of two years duration. 25% of student time over the four years of undergraduate programmes and 40% of student time over the two years of postgraduate programmes should be allocated to school placement' (ibid.: 12). This means that, typically, a student teacher in Ireland will spend in the region of twenty weeks in schools over the course of those programmes. In all cases, the second half of the program must include one ten-week block placement.

Fancourt et al. (2015) provide a good overview of the situation in UK teacher education, while Conway et al. (2009) examine the Irish context and compare the practices in nine countries: England, Scotland, Northern Ireland, Finland, New Zealand, Singapore, United States and Poland. Their comprehensive report informed school placement policy of the Teaching Council of Ireland. Mattsson et al. (2011) explain the process in Australia, Canada, Sweden, China, Norway, Denmark, Finland and the Netherlands.

## *Some challenges*

The concern shared in most contexts is summed up by Feiman-Nemser (2001: 1013–4) when she says:

> If we want schools to produce more powerful learning on the part of students we have to offer more powerful learning opportunities to teachers. Conventional programmes of teacher education and professional development are not designed to promote complex learning by teachers or students. The typical preservice program is a weak intervention compared with the influence of teachers' own schooling and their on-the-job experience.

We authors feel that if host schools, school placement tutors and ITE education departments were to engage in professional development that would enable them to collaborate in self-study action research undertaken by student teachers while on placement, it might result in a more beneficial partnership for all involved including, importantly, the schoolchildren. From our experience it certainly engages the student teachers. 'Involving students in inquiry – in research – is a way of improving their learning, motivating them more. After all, what motivates large numbers of academics is engaging in the excitement of research' (Jenkins et al. 2003: ix). Seeking to enhance the school placement experience for the student teacher and the cooperating school is no small task for an ITE provider. Schools are pressurized contexts, and teachers, especially those of examination classes, can be reluctant to relinquish control of their classes to undergraduates. As Feiman-Nemser states:

> Teacher education students regard student teaching as the most valuable part of their preparation … At the same time cooperating teachers often feel the need to protect student teachers from 'impractical' ideas promoted by education professors who are out of touch with classroom realities. When the people responsible for field experiences do not work closely with the people who teach academic and professional courses, there is no

productive joining of forces around a common agenda and no sharing of expertise. (Feiman-Nemser 2001: 1020)

Therefore there are both challenges and advantages to the school placement process for all stakeholders, and these vary between colleges and universities in individual countries. Day and Sachs (2004: 15) suggest that effective partnerships are based on reciprocity 'where both parties meet on equal grounds, with the desire to improve student learning outcomes and teaching practice at its core'. However, no one can improve another person: we can only seek to improve what we do ourselves and we then hope that our changed practice will have a positive educational influence in other people's learning. On that basis, we authors argue that an invitational and collaborative self-study approach may provide a foundation for reciprocal, effective partnerships. We bear in mind Russell's (2002: 74) statement about the concept of a school–university partnership having 'an elusive and amorphous quality that is frequently sought and infrequently achieved'.

Examining the UK experience, Greany et al. (2014) suggest that national policy regarding school placement is, in many contexts, incoherent and fragmented. On the plus side, they say, are the potentially enriching learning opportunities for student teachers and teacher educators, as well as for the cooperating teachers in the schools (Bolton 2014; Scaife 2009). Like Zeichner (2010), Greany et al. (2014: 6) state that 'successful partnerships often appear to succeed by creating "a third space" which is separate from the culture of either institution and allows for more creative ways of working'. For Greany and Brown (2015) this third space may mean that schools need to develop a deeper relationship with a college or university, where time and space is provided for staff from each institution to work together to achieve agreed objectives. In my college we sought to create such a third space by seeking to build researcherly dispositions (Lingard and Renshaw 2010) – particularly action-researcherly dispositions (Sullivan et al. 2016) among student teachers. Lingard and Renshaw (2010: 37) suggest that practitioners, policymakers and teachers should all be interested in research and knowledge production, and see themselves as participants in the field of educational research: that is, educational professionals should be 'research-informed, but also research-informing' (ibid.).

# Reflective opportunity

Outline what you understand by a school–university partnership.
Who do you consider are the main stakeholders?
Describe some of the challenges and advantages to the placement
   process.

# Case study: offering a model of SSAR for establishing a researcherly disposition

Let's now examine how we tried to establish a researcherly disposition in a small college in terms of *context; the relationship between SSAR and principles of constructivist, active learning; the reflective practitioner model for student teachers; and new forms of knowing for undergraduates.*

## *Context*

The college in which I work provides a four-year concurrent degree that focuses on preparing students for teaching in post-primary schools. Our college is small and our programmes are accredited by a larger university. At the time of writing we are an autonomous private college but plans are afoot to have us incorporated into, and become a remote campus of, a larger college of education and thus, course modules may change.

Our students are encouraged from the beginning of their course to engage in personal and professional development, which we hope will encourage them to become responsible and critically reflective practitioners. We are a relatively new (2004) institution, and staff work collegially across the four departments to advocate student-centred teaching and learning. Student teachers are evaluated on their teaching placements: they are given verbal and written feedback on the day of their inspections and also via email correspondence throughout their placement, as well as while meeting their tutor for a post-placement meeting. After two placements, students are generally very well aware of their own strengths and shortcomings. Through reflecting on the areas in which they feel they need to improve, they arrive at the end of their third year with a strong sense of where to focus their final year self-study research project. Tutors may point them towards areas for improvement but, ultimately, the student decides on the area of focus. This is an important aspect of the self-study process, as was pointed out in Chapter 1. It is always a source of satisfaction for me to see the clarity with which most students face their research.

In the college also, there are some staff members who engage in action research. Regular faculty meetings are held, during which we conduct 'professional conversations' (Clark 2001) to review and modify our practice. I have been involved in providing professional development for staff and for school placement tutors, in constructivist learning approaches and in developing an understanding of self-study action research values. An open and accountable culture enables us to try to ensure that constructivist principles are promoted across all programmes. I like to think too, that my background and experience in self-study action research has enabled me to have an educative influence (McNiff and Whitehead 2009) in my institution, which is forward thinking and creative (see Roche 2014).

## *Active learning*

In Roche (2014) I explained how I feel that it would be incongruous to lecture students propositionally about constructivism, and therefore I have tried to model constructivist approaches in my teaching and incorporate active learning opportunities throughout all my modules. The epistemological foundation for a constructivist approach is that knowledge is created by knowers for themselves, through building on prior knowledge. Learning is active, social and contextual, and knowledge is always partial and evolving. This epistemological foundation fits well with the epistemological values of self-study. Self-study action research is also premised on the idea that we must constantly engage in robust, active and critical reflection on our practice (see Sullivan et al. 2016). Because of this, I sought to develop an authentic, critically reflective aspect for my students' final year project that would engage them in examining their own practice. Drawing on Douglas and Ellis (2011: 175), my colleagues and I sought to rethink 'both the social relationships and the processes of abstracting knowledge from experience ... as we endeavour to enhance the learning' of our student teachers. The reflective process is encouraged and developed throughout each year, currently culminating (in the education component), in the self-study action research project in Year 4. Despite the hard work involved, student feedback has been very positive:

> My teaching philosophy has been influenced by many factors: my own school experience, my current teaching experience, and my educational experiences in college. It was refined during my work on my Self-Study Action Research, (SSAR), whereby, through self-reflection, I identified the teaching values that I deem to be at the centre of my teaching philosophy. My SSAR taught me the value of self-reflection. Through this reflection I can improve my teaching, my learning, and potentially, the students' learning. I can state that my SSAR improved how I view my practice. It compelled me to analyse how my personal values are translated into professional values, and how I can genuinely live these values. I was able to demonstrate to myself times when these values were upheld or not upheld through examined evidence from my School Placements. It was a very personal learning experience for me. (From Year 4 student's Professional Portfolio, May 2016)

Now let's take a closer look at what is involved over the four-year programme and the relevance this has for the school–college partnership.

## The reflective practitioner model in the education component

In Roche (2014) I explained how first-year students are encouraged, from the outset, to see themselves as education researchers and to view any reflective assignments as a form, albeit basic, of education research. In Foundations of Education modules, students are introduced to the principles underpinning learner-centred teaching and to pedagogical relationships grounded in Buber's (1958) I–Thou theory. They are also introduced to Whitehead's (1993) Living Educational Theory and begin the first phase of reflective writing about their teaching philosophy as they develop their professional portfolio.

In their second year, students build on this portfolio. Following their first school placement, they are supported in becoming critical (Carr and Kemmis 1986) as they begin to examine the complexity of the field of education and to scrutinize some of their assumptions about teaching, learning and students. They are introduced to the notion of critical reflection on practice (Sullivan et al. 2016) through engaging with Brookfield's (1995; 2012) ideas.

In Year 3, students continue to develop their professional portfolio and begin to undertake a two-year engagement with self-study action research. At this stage they are asked to examine their educational values and to identify an area of concern, based on school placement experiences and tutor evaluations, which might merit more careful scrutiny. This culminates in researching the literatures around their chosen area. Rather than being seen as a traditional literature review, their assignment is titled 'How do I deepen my understanding of …'

In their fourth and final year, students revisit their area of concern and use their final school placement setting as a site for critical reflection and action as they examine their practice in a critical, reflective and reflexive manner through a self-study action research approach, grounded in Whitehead's (1993) living theory principles.

More recently another element has been added in the form of an annual Education Symposium. This is held a month or so after school placement ends. Students from Year 2 present posters on elements of their professional portfolios; Year 3 present their initial research into the literatures and conceptual frameworks of the area of their practice which they intend to investigate in Year 4. Year 4 students present their learning from their SSAR. Invitations are issued to all principals of local schools, to cooperating teachers of school placement sites, and to tutors and college staff. External academics with expertise in SSAR interview the Year 4 students and evaluate their posters. The posters are also subjected to peer evaluation whereby each student is interviewed by three peers who select two aspects of the poster/research as being positive, and one aspect as meriting clarification, improvement or development. A self-evaluative element is in place in that students write a reflection on their learning from the event for their professional portfolio. The Education Symposium affords Year 4 students an alternative form of representation of their research account to the traditional written form and presents an opportunity for students from Years 2 and 3 to become familiar with the SSAR process. Here is one final year student's reflection:

> The concept of Self-Study Action Research took me a long time to grasp. For the Education Symposium in my Year Three (2015), I presented the findings of my literature review. Whilst I understood the concept of why I had undertaken the literature review, I was still very unsure of how I would put my findings into practice. My greatest struggle is that I find reflection very private. I struggled to gain confidence in putting my work on display: what if I am wrong, or I have deviated, or I am making unfounded claims? After the Education Symposium in 2015, I felt I had gained some insight.... I spoke about the values that underpin my teaching. My examiner asked about my values. Could I give further examples of how my values are evident in my teaching? I provided a clear and passionate answer; not an answer where I was portraying myself as brilliant, but an answer where I demonstrated my struggle in that the school placement was only five weeks long. I am worried that perhaps for five weeks I can uphold these values, but in the long term can I still maintain them? The examiner stated 'be gentle on yourself'. This was a real, genuine piece of learning for me. Dewey recognised that the main aim of education was growth and deemed that growth occurs in the process of putting ideas to the test of experience. I may struggle through my first few years as an NQT. However, if I continue to reflect and to strive to test my ideas and ideals, perhaps I will grow professionally. (From Year 4 student's Professional Portfolio, May 2016)

## *New form of knowing for undergraduates*

In Roche (2014) I described how many students struggle to see themselves as knowers in third level. Because of this, some find it difficult to understand the principles of SSAR which some perceive as being grounded in a radical and new approach to knowledge and knowing. After all, these students have recently emerged from a post-primary setting largely premised on Freire's (1970) 'banking model' and so, their previous experience of education has been largely that of receiver of others' knowledge. Now they are being asked to see themselves as generators of educational knowledge, even theory, as they seek to improve their own practice. As well, up to this point in college, apart from their reflective journal assignments, they have been required to use the third-person passive voice in written academic work. This switch of focus to 'I, and me, and my practice' (in an assignment which, at the time of writing, is worth 40% of a 10-credit module) can be destabilizing and risky for many students.

We will now examine how this process has impacted on the school placement practicum and its implications for school–college partnerships.

# The SSAR approach: The potential significance; the epistemological, ontological and methodological challenges for the school–college partnership

The process of engaging in SSAR to support the school–college partnership is not without challenges in the school placement process. As we will see, these are mainly to do with the *epistemological, ontological and methodological* principles of the approach, which I will discuss below. Yet we authors believe that addressing these challenges can be potentially empowering for all involved.

First-year students carry out classroom observation in senior primary school settings. They are encouraged to write reflectively about different aspects of teaching and learning: on the way classrooms are organized, the questioning styles, different teaching approaches, how learners engage and more. They are also encouraged to engage in dialogue with the classroom teacher and other school personnel about different teaching and learning issues. This has several areas worthy of development. How might the cooperating school staff members become more engaged with the process? What is the potential significance for their CPD? Drawing on Sugrue et al. (2001), we could ask how the process might become more facilitative, empowering and supportive for them. We authors suggest that the key host school staff – those with direct involvement with the student teacher in particular– would be offered, by the ITE provider, a short piece of professional development in the principles of self-study action research (Glenn et al. 2012: 29). This CPD could enable host school staff to act as confident critical friends for the student teachers as they go about their work and their classroom observations.

During their following three years the student teachers engage in school placements in post-primary settings. As stated previously, they conduct their self-study action research enquiry during their final placement. School placement is a collaborative process: researching practice in a school context involves many different kinds of documentation: lesson plans, schemes of work, reflections, and evaluations, for example. These documents can serve as data-gathering opportunities. This immediately involves others, such as pupils, tutors, peers, cooperating teachers and principals, as participants, collaborators and critical friends. The ethics statement and permission request, submitted to the school authorities in advance of the placement, emphasizes that the student is not carrying out research 'on' the school or 'on' the pupils, but that the research is a self-study focussing on the student teacher's own practice. Again, there is partnership potential here. The ITE College could provide in-service on the underpinning principles and methodological features of SSAR. The school staff could reciprocate by providing input on their ethos, mission, curricular features and pedagogy. They would also be in a strong position to act as mentors and critical friends for the student teachers as they research their practice, as Zeichner (2010) suggested.

## *Epistemological assumptions*

One of the biggest epistemological hurdles I encounter, as I try to prepare both students and school placement tutors for the self-study process, is their view of what counts as valid research (Roche 2014). Many tutors even question whether the knowledge that is generated through a self-study action research approach (by our students or by any undergraduates) could be considered valid knowledge. This view is largely grounded in the positivist paradigm of which Bernie wrote in Chapter 4, where researchers objectively study phenomena, and where the research is considered valid only when it is replicable and generalizable. My experience has been that some students and tutors, particularly those who may have higher degrees grounded in traditional epistemology, find it hard to accept that a study of the self by the self can be valid. This may also be true of cooperating school staff members. As I promote a self-study action research approach, that I hope will contribute to 'fluidising historical and cultural boundaries' (Whitehead 2013: 1) between what some understand as research, and what self-study can offer them in terms of realizing their educational values in their practice, I draw on the work of McNiff (2013), Reason and Bradbury (2013) and Whitehead (2013), in explaining my rationale.

The primary purpose of action research, according to Reason and Bradbury (2013: 4), is to produce practical knowing 'in the pursuit of worthwhile human purposes'. Action research, they suggest, is about working towards practical outcomes, and also about creating new forms of understanding, 'since action without reflection and understanding is blind, just as theory without action is meaningless' (ibid.). These epistemological perspectives suggest that self-study action research is grounded in ways of thinking and knowing that view any knowledge generated in such enquiries as partial, incomplete and provisional, a process of coming to know, rather than a reified product. This means that the findings of such research cannot be readily generalizable or replicable. Douglas and Ellis (2011: 175) suggest that, institutionally, universities and schools are required to work with 'different conceptual tool-kits'. Students and other stakeholders, who have long been exposed to valuing abstract knowledge (or assessable/measureable knowledge) over practical knowing, can find the transition from one epistemological 'tool-kit' to another particularly difficult (Roche 2014).

## *Ontological perspectives*

Ontology influences how we see ourselves and others, and is described in McNiff (2013: 27) as 'the way we view ourselves, a theory of being'. In Roche (2014) I wrote about how the ontological assumptions of school placement can present us with several different challenges. Stakeholders in the school–college partnership need to be cognizant of the challenges presented by the fact that, while on placement, some students can find the competing identities of being both a student and a teacher to be a very difficult concept to grapple with.

Our students have been exposed since their first-year education modules to Buber's (1958) I–Thou theory, which underpins the implications of saying, for example, 'We do not talk about studying the children in Class A1. We talk instead about studying *our teaching* in collaboration *with* the children in A1; we do not study differentiation, we study *our teaching* as we seek to differentiate.' Where epistemological and ontological areas are entwined with methodological issues in this way, there is a risk of confusion. For many students, although self-study appeared to have made sense in theory, during their preparation lectures and workshops, in practice several still felt they were 'researching pupils' or 'researching an issue'. Likewise, some tutors supporting them failed to recognize when the student drifted into an outsider-researcher perspective. We authors argue for a more in-depth process of professional development for tutors and cooperating teachers in host schools, and some of these dilemmas might be avoided.

## *Methodology*

In Roche (2014) I explained how I drew on Whitehead's action reflection cycles (Whitehead 1989) and on McDonagh et al. (2012) to inform the questions, ideas and actions with which the students were encouraged to engage. Questions of the type 'What am I doing?' and 'Why am I doing it?' gave a living form to the students' educational enquiries. They begin by asking: How do I improve what I am doing? How do I live my values more fully in my practice? (Whitehead 1993). Most students genuinely seek to engage with these reflective and reflexive questions and most succeed. The potential significance for education in general, as well as for the school–college partnerships, is evident in student reflections. Here are some examples:

1. My SSAR forced me to ask myself some tough questions: What do I believe in and how can I act upon my educational beliefs? These were not easily answered questions; I am a lifelong people pleaser, as a result I continually had to ask myself, do I really value X or am I just saying that because it is the socially correct answer? This resulted in me gaining confidence in what I do really value. I tried so many teaching strategies throughout my school placements, questioning if the students were learning. I care about the answer to that question. I respect their desire to learn. I can uphold my beliefs through differentiation. These statements are all assertions due to my participation in my SSAR; they will underpin my professional life.

2. On a personal level, my research made me stop and think about the career path that I have chosen. During my 4th year school placement I aimed to lead the lifestyle I hope to lead during my career. It was the first time that I genuinely faced up to the fact that in order to uphold my educational values, my personal time will be affected: I am happy with that. My personal and educational values certainly blend into one another.

3. If I am to improve my teaching skills, I will need to be a part of a cycle of continuous professional development, where I can learn new skills and incorporate these skills into the learning environment. Research suggests that the more control a teacher has over their CPD the more likely they are to learn from it and find it effective for both their personal and professional development. (From Year 4 students' Professional Portfolios, May 2016)

As they begin to articulate their values and see them embodied in their practice, the students have demonstrated that they are boundary-crossers. They have begun the transition from a student identity to a more professional teacher identity. This growing professionalism has come about, we authors believe, because the students owned their learning: they focused on a concern that they identified and chose to study, rather than on a topic selected for them and imposed by others. This is key to the process and cannot be underestimated or should not be compromised. It would need to be a core part of any CPD for stakeholders.

# The potential learning for participating student teachers and education lecturers

In this section I will explore, through case studies, the significance of the self-study action research process for *students*. I will then examine the potential significance for *college lecturers, school–college partnerships, school placement tutors and whole-school staffs.*

## The significance of the self-study action research process for students

The following case studies provide further examples of the kinds of concerns about their practice that students identified as areas for research. I chose to highlight the work of these three students because they have already made their accounts public (see also Roche 2011; 2014). These successes have significance for the learning of both student teachers and education lecturers alike and, perhaps, potential significance for policymakers.

## Case studies

The professional concern bothering Paul was in relation to his use of ICT in his final school placement setting. As Paul examined his values, he began to realize that he had been singled out for praise by tutors in earlier placements because of his proficiency with ICT. His self-study research process led him to an understanding that he had begun to reify ICT as a product that allowed him to demonstrate expertise – a chance to shine as a teacher – rather than as an educational resource for enhancing pupil learning. His research account demonstrated a high level of critical reflection.

While in third year, Jim's area of concern was in relation to school drop-out rates. His choice of 'retention rates in post-primary contexts' as his area of literature research drew on the fact that he was dismayed, when on his Year 3 placement in a disadvantaged school setting, to find that many of the students he had taught in Junior Cycle, in his Year 2 placement, had not returned for the Senior Cycle. While researching such an issue might result in improved propositional knowledge about why some adolescents drop out of school, it might not have impacted in any real way on Jim's practice. Jim realized that he needed to address his own teaching. Following reflection, he realized that change must begin in himself. This resulted in the title of his self-study evolving to: 'How can I teach in a way that will not exclude or marginalize any child?' He saw that he needed to challenge both his understanding and practice around issues of equity so as to engage in authentic inclusion.

Rachel is arty and creative. She values emancipatory, innovative teaching methodologies. She felt that she needed to understand why, in final year post-primary classes, she found it easier to use creative approaches in her teaching of Religious Education (which was not an exam subject) than in her teaching of *Gaeilge* (the Irish language, which, for most students, was a compulsory exam subject). Rachel's enquiry led her to new understandings of democratic practice that suited the learning needs of her pupils rather than her own creative teaching needs. She also demonstrated that for her, critical reflection has become a reflexive way of being and has left her with a conviction that self-study action research is an authentic and effective approach to CPD.

## *Transformative learning for students*

These three students, along with their peers, generated a theory of practice that is personally and professionally valid. They created what Whitehead (2013) suggests are valid explanations for the educational influences in their own learning, in the learning of others and in the learning of the social formations in which they live and work. These three students were and are 'willing to hold themselves to account for living their values of humanity as fully as possible in enquiries of the kind, "How do I improve what I am doing?" ' (Whitehead 2013: 6.) They each chose a personal area of concern that was grounded in their own unique educational values. They designed original ways of collaborating with their colleagues, pupils and critical friends; original ways of gathering data and original ways of generating evidence using their unique values as criteria and standards of judgement (Whitehead and McNiff 2006: 7). I would argue that their learning was transformative in nature: they each wrote in their accounts that they now think differently and they each said they will continue to ground their CPD in a self-reflective and self-evaluative approach. For example, Jim said:

It would have been much easier to just do research on 'Retention in the Post-Primary sector'. A bit of reading and writing and thinking would be all that was needed and then I could go on with my life. This action research showed me that I can't just study something 'out there'. After doing even this small bit of self-study research, I see now that the buck stops here – with me. I'm 'it': I have to take responsibility for being the best teacher

I can be, for being the most inclusive and just teacher I can be. It's not good enough anymore to go into the staff room and say 'I can't teach them: they don't even speak English'. I have to do something about it. (Conversation with Jim, June 2013).

Each student documented and disseminated their understanding of the transformation they had brought about in their own learning. Each has come to the understanding that reflection must be authentic and personal rather than a prescribed exercise. In a conversation about reflection and the written reflective assignments included in school placement requirements, Jim said:

We had to write something, so what I did was I'd go back over my lecture notes and find something like 'Positive Discipline' and then I'd weave something together using some theory or other from lectures. I'd fill my required number of words and print it out and bang it into my folder. No way was it real reflection. After doing the action research, I know better now. (Conversation with Jim, June 2013)

Their self-study action research became an opportunity for students to generate knowledge for themselves. Because I firmly believe that all education should aim to be transformative in nature, I genuinely sought to develop ways of enabling the assignment to be grounded in constructivist epistemological and ontological principles, and the values of Whitehead's (1989) living educational theory. Transformation cannot be forced on anyone. Those students who were open to and committed to the self-study action research process found out for themselves that transformation happened when they honestly sought change in their practice and their thinking about practice.

## *Further significance of the self-study action research process for students*

Jim, Rachel and Paul made their work open and accountable when they presented their accounts of living their educational theories at an International Research Methodologies Summer School (June 2013). Comments after their presentations included: 'I am so glad I came along this morning. Your idealism, enthusiasm and honesty remind us all of why we became teachers'; 'These students demonstrate that they are reflective and reflexive practitioners who have engaged with the ideas, tried to improve as teachers and have generated a personal theory of teaching and learning' (see Roche 2014).

These were comments made by people who generally shared my epistemological values. However, a science teacher studying for his PhD said, 'I'm more of a stats man myself but I was impressed by the presenters. They gave very credible accounts of how their eyes were opened to the complexities of what happens in classrooms – some of which, I suppose, is not quantifiable', which would appear that he considers the knowledge generated by the three students to be valid even though it was not supported by his particular epistemological values. He did not appear to be aware that action research holds an inclusive stance in relation to data-gathering, and action researchers do not exclude statistical or empirical data.

## Potential significance for college lecturers

The annual education symposia provided college staff with an opportunity to view SSAR projects and interview the students. Several college staff members provided positive feedback and were frank about the fact that prior to the first symposium they were sceptical but viewing the students' work had convinced them of the worth of the process:

> This is the most authentic critical reflection I have ever seen undergraduates carry out.
>
> You could tell by the students that they genuinely 'get it' – they really 'live' and love their research.
>
> I was amazed at how few chose to study classroom discipline or classroom management – that was my own biggest concern when I was a student teacher.
>
> These students studied a very diverse range of topics but each one was personal to themselves – it was real to them.
>
> I was quite interested in the seamless way they spoke about philosophers, theories and practice as they explained the values base of their study. (Staff Evaluation, May 2015/6)

## Potential Significance for School–College partnerships

There is scope here for developing the model further to allow for genuine reciprocity and collaborative practice in school–college partnerships. However, its design will demand some tweaking in relation to school placement tutors/ supervisors, in-house staff and host school staff. Professional development will be central. All stakeholders will require in-service in the principles of self-study action research. In return, host schools can provide professional development for student teachers and school placement tutors. We have looked at the process from the point of view of the ITE staff. Now let's briefly examine how supervisors/tutors and host school staff might be involved.

## *School placement tutor*

Supervision, according to Bolton (2014: 58) is a 'form of experiential learning that supports reflective examination of practice … [and is] an intensely interpersonally focussed one-to-one relationship'. Citing Scaife (2009: x) she says that 'supervisees open up their work and their committed behaviours, performance, practice, writing, thinking and feelings, to scrutiny by another. Judgements will be made, usually by a person with greater experience and often in the context of a formal power relationship.' Ong'ondo and Jwan (2009: 517) explain that the main goal of supervision should be 'to support novice teachers to form the correct mental disposition and be ready to improve during the time'. They also argue that such support is important because the 'journey novice teachers experience is especially intense, conflicting, dynamic and fragile (ibid.).

The supervisor–supervisee relationship, we feel, is ideal for supporting a student engaged in self-study action research where the tutor can act as a critical friend and mentor alongside their evaluative role. However it does mean that the tutor must have a good working knowledge of the principles of self-study and shares the epistemological values of the research approach. Many tutors are former or retired school principals or teachers: they will be au fait with current practices and policy in relation to school self-evaluation. It is not too big a step for them to grapple with the methodology and philosophical base of self-study. It would be prudent however for the host ITE College to provide CPD for the tutors. This done, the tutor is in a strong position to provide valuable advice and ask critical questions of the student.

# Reflective opportunity

What are the challenges presented by involving supervisors and
    supervisees in self-study?
What are the advantages?

## *Cooperating teacher and host school staff*

Many teachers are actively engaged in professional development and are au fait with new policies and thinking about education. Rorrison (2011: 40) suggests that 'with more and more teachers in schools maintaining the currency of their professional knowledge through further study and research, it may be time to put more value on their role as teacher educators and educational leaders'. Conversations between student teachers (who have access to recent developments in the theoretical aspects of education generally, and in pedagogy in particular) and teachers in situ in host schools (who have the live up-to-date knowledge of practice, as well as knowledge garnered through professional development) could be mutually beneficial. Cooperative, reflective, professional conversations of the type envisioned by Clark (2001) could be developed. Groundwater-Smith et al. (1997), in a similar vein, argue that workplace learning for teachers in situ can also be seen as a form of practicum where a professional learning conversation about practice can take place. We argue that if host school staff members were to be offered professional development in the principles and practice of SSAR, and if they were prepared to examine their own practice alongside the student teacher, it could serve as useful professional learning for them, along with a means of supporting and mentoring student teachers (Glenn et al. 2012). Loughran (2002) argues that self-study allows teacher educators 'to better understand the nature of teaching about teaching and to develop a genuine sense of professional satisfaction in that work' as well as 'to maintain a focus on their teaching and on their student's learning' (ibid.: 245). Because these are high priorities in teacher education, he argues that 'thus self-study complements their work. As a result, a most valuable aspect of self-study is apparent in the development of ways of knowing, or the professional knowledge of teaching and learning about teaching' (ibid.).

## To conclude

We agree with Russell (2002) who argues that self-study is a way for teacher educators to reframe and respond to their practice. We suggest that a combined self-study approach between student teachers, teacher educators, supervisors/tutors, and cooperating teachers could bring about a realization of a genuine school–college partnership in Zeichner's (2010) 'third space' to which we already referred, and could go some way towards dispelling some of the amorphous qualities of the partnership that were alluded to earlier. We recognize that this is not without challenges for teacher unions and regulatory bodies as well as the relevant stakeholders, but we consider it worth the effort. It could be argued that the wider school–college partnership can be seen as representing a community of learners, or a professional learning group, that relies on mutual respect, professional conversations and authentic dialogue, as we have outlined throughout the book.

# 7

# Tapping into Experiential Knowledge in Whole-School Communities

## *Caitriona McDonagh*

## Introduction

The school placement experience described in the previous chapter can present challenges for teachers in schools. In our experience the underlying difficulty for teachers is that they rarely have opportunities to articulate the wealth of knowledge that they can bring to such learning partnerships. This chapter follows our journey of encouraging teachers to appreciate their experiential and professional knowledge. This involved facilitating action research among whole-school staff learning communities. The journey goes from initiating learning communities within whole schools, to enabling staff, both as individuals and as members of a collaborative group, to conduct action research into their practice.

In this chapter I explore:

- looking at relationships within whole-school learning communities

- encouraging participant involvement in whole-school learning communities

- supporting participants' freedom to own their professional knowledge

- supporting the evaluation of teaching

- examining the importance of tapping into teachers' individual experiential and professional knowledge.

## Relationships within whole-school learning communities

My personal commitment to the idea of whole-school learning communities developed during my classroom research (McDonagh 2007). I drew on the insights I gained from my classroom learning community and utilized them as I convened whole-school staff learning communities. As I carried out my classroom research, I saw how my class became a learning community as the students and I engaged in dialogue around their learning. A video clip from that research encapsulated for me the significance of setting up a learning community within a classroom, as you will see in the following example.

> When I was researching my teaching of pupils with specific learning disability (dyslexia), I encouraged them to research their own understanding of their specific difficulties in learning. They then presented their reports to their peers and teachers. A video-clip shows how these young presenters interacted with groups of peers, their class teacher, a student teacher on school placement, a classroom assistant, the School Head and me – their learning support teacher. Each presenter explained their report to a group of four other pupils plus a staff member. The video-clip shows all of them seriously engaged as a learning group – listening, questioning and evaluating their new learning. (Based on Roche et al. 2010)

Reflecting on the embryonic learning community in the video, I identified some key traits that are common to effective learning communities. They included *relationships, motivation, freedom, validity and the recognition of participants as valued experts* (Roche et al. 2010), each of which I will explain. Based on my experiences of working with whole-school educational learning communities, I believe that these characteristics are needed to support such communities.

*Relationships*: The video clip clearly showed that pupils who presented their reports were no longer perceived as less able. They were competently answering questions such as, 'When did you realize that you read so slowly? Did your slow reading stop you from learning other subjects? Which subjects?' In the video clip everyone in the room appeared to be fully engrossed in a learning process. There was an equality in the relationships growing in the group. I believe that this equality can best be seen in the nature of the dialogue that occurred.

*Motivation*: Positive experiences can motivate learning. This can be seen in the video clip when the presenters stood in front of the class and answered questions from everyone in the room. I wrote, 'Pupil H smiles as she skips back to her seat, applause from me, the School Head and the whole class ringing in her ears' (McDonagh 2007: 206). This pupil wrote about her experience as follows: 'I want to research more and explain dyslexia to myself and everyone else' (Video transcript McDonagh 2007).

*Freedom*: Both the children and adults in the video clip had the freedom to learn in whatever mode suited them – looking, listening, reflecting, asking questions to clarify or making links to their prior understanding of dyslexia, retelling others what they had learned, making notes or doodles to help them remember as they learned. At the request of their peers, the presenters moved from group to group so that the whole class of pupils and teachers could recap and compare what they learned. This decision showed that individually and as a learning community they took responsibility for their own learning and they acted on it. The freedom to take responsibility for one's learning is imperative in communities of learning.

*Validity*: Learning communities can validate new learning. The video clip showed how the presenters made public their claims to new knowledge about their capability to learn. An example of how the group validated their claims was when the school head said, at the end of the video clip, 'I can only say that I compliment you (the presenters) for your courage – courage in talking to us (as he points to the staff in the room) and showing us how difficult we can make learning for you; courage also in knowing that each day life in school will be hard for you as you try to find your own ways to learn' (Video transcript McDonagh 2007).

*Participants as valued experts*: It should be borne in mind that the presenters described here were children who had been officially labelled as learning disabled, whose voices would not normally be heard. They were now shown as valued experts who contributed to the learning of all in the room. For example, one of the teachers present wrote, 'I learned a lot about dyslexia. There were certain things I hadn't realised. I think I would now do things differently for children with dyslexia in the class' (McDonagh 2007: 261). I believe that it is necessary to be open to accepting all participants in learning communities as valued experts who can make worthwhile contributions.

When I began to work with whole-school learning communities, I decided to maintain the key features of *relationships, motivation, freedom, validity and the recognition of participants as valued experts* that I had observed in my classroom community and transfer them into adult communities. I now choose these five features as my chapter subheadings to explain the creation of effective whole-school learning communities.

## Establishing whole-school learning communities

Sometime after the classroom research above, and building on our work with the Teaching Council of Ireland (Glenn et al. 2012), we authors supported whole-school staffs in a self-evaluation process. In one such school the principal knew that his staff had evaluated pupil learning. They had conducted pupil standardized tests at each class level and compiled detailed profiles for pupils with special learning needs. But staff had never discussed the implications of these well-documented evaluations for the management and resourcing of the schools' teaching. Staff meetings had been for information delivery rather than discussion. So a starting point of my learning journey was to find how best to encourage this learning community to engage in more open and collaborative conversations and utilize the knowledge they already held. What happened reinforced for me the importance of the idea of equality in relationships in such learning communities, as you will see in the following examples from the two schools.

## School One

Below I explain what happened when we invited staff in one school to complete a cycle of action research over the course of a year. Since the school head and deputy head were concerned about the quality of staff communications, we discussed how we might enhance staff engagement. At my initial meeting with the whole-school staff of forty, we gathered in a cramped classroom after school. Initially there was an air of polite tiredness. I invited them to join in whole-school self-evaluation through a process of reflection, action and evaluation. I will explain later in this chapter how they became sufficiently motivated, despite their fatigue, to unanimously agree, in writing, to begin the process at our next two-hour meeting. For now, I want to focus on the relationship that developed between the school head, deputy head and myself.

I found that our dialogues captured our growing relationship. Between staff meetings, as we discussed how we might encourage collaborative participation, we critically reflected and took action based on our evaluations. We realized that in our interactions we were modelling the collegiality and the open, constructive relationship that we hoped to promote among the whole-school staff. We decided to continue this model of open discussion and action into the meetings with staff by encouraging honest and open dialogue. We did this in a number of ways – for example, in each session, we invited staff to comment on how they felt about the process honestly and openly. We made opportunities for a wide variety of collaborative actions where staff could discuss their successes as well as their concerns. In doing so they gained encouragement from one another. Here is what the school head said about his staff's interactions, 'When we began, people were a little wary. But they gradually realised that we were helping each other. We were actually learning to open up to each other for the first time' (Transcript from video, September 2012). He was demonstrating the importance of equality in relationships that is necessary to generate open conversations. In this scenario, the benefits of being creative in modelling and encouraging openness and equality in dialogue became obvious. Although I was convinced of the need to support open conversations and more equal dialogue in effective learning communities, this was not always possible, as you will see in an example from another school.

## *School Two*

On this occasion, the whole-school staff were working on areas they had each personally chosen and were collecting data for their individual projects. Then something unusual happened. The school head decided that instead of teachers pursuing their individual areas of interest, they were all to work on numeracy and specifically on problem solving. Unfortunately, his controlling of the process ended what had been a collegial learning group where relationships were developing as all participants worked together. While the school head may have been influenced by anticipated government requirements in relation to forthcoming National Literacy and Numeracy Initiatives (Ireland, Department of Education and Skills 2011), he disempowered his staff by deciding to impose his choice of a specific curriculum focus. Staff now realized that they were not valued as experts. The imposition of one focus for the whole group meant they were denied important opportunities to draw on their own values, and to critically reflect on, and evaluate, their priorities as teaching and learning professionals. The open conversations and equality in their developing relationships had been severed as a new power dynamic was imposed on the group.

As a facilitator of whole-school learning communities, I see my role as a gate opener. I look for routes to more open conversations about teaching and learning for all. However, as you have seen, in the examples above, school management and leaders can become gatekeepers for new knowledge creation for whole-school communities. So it is essential for them to support and understand the underlying thinking of an action research approach. In most cases this can best be done by school leaders seeing themselves as active participants in the whole-school learning community. Likewise, in school–college partnerships, college staff may hold the gate open, ajar or closed to effective learning communities. Our research and experience found that this gate opening requires building relationships through dialogue. The forms of dialogue we recommend have been discussed in Chapter 1 and are part of what Buber (1958) referred to as I–Thou relationships where we are engaging with each other's whole being. When I am establishing a whole-school learning community, I reflect on and examine participants' dialogue for examples of equality in the contributions made because this is an indicator of the healthy state of the group's relationships. This mirrors what I observed many years earlier in the classroom learning community, as I described in the beginning of this chapter.

In whole-school learning communities, school leaders often find it challenging to walk the fine line between government control and school-based initiatives (Hairona and Dimmock 2014). In response to such challenges, here is a summary of the effective actions that we have learned from our work with whole-school learning communities:

- model the process of collegial action
- build on positives
- be creative in finding opportunities for members to work collaboratively
- acknowledge embodied values
- engage in self-evaluation (this includes myself, as facilitator, and school leaders)
- be aware of power issues.

I now invite educational and learning community leaders to consider those possible actions as they think about the following questions.

## Reflective opportunity

How might you set up professional, collegial relationships?
How might you find ways to acknowledge positives within a professional
    learning community?
How can gatekeepers be encouraged to trust the autonomy and agency
    of staff members?
Do you need to change your ways of facilitating or teaching in order to
    bring all participants together into school learning communities?

# Encouraging participants to become fully involved in whole-school learning communities

Motivation is key in encouraging participants to engage in whole-school learning communities and an initial challenge for me, as a facilitator, was how to engage the teachers who were not fully on board. In my experience of working with school staff, there were often staff members who were not interested in listening to required professional development input. There were also those who had worked competently in isolation and saw no need for working as a community. A first step in the process of motivating participants to articulate their professional knowledge was to encourage whole-school communities to reflect and evaluate together. This meant talking about the practical, real-life experiences of their teaching situation, reflecting on them alone and as a whole group so as to develop the necessary vocabulary to articulate their professional knowledge. Here is an example of how I recorded the beginning of one such process:

A day's work over. As I walked in trepidation into a classroom of staff members, an aura of uncommunicativeness hit me. How was I going to break through this barrier? As an ice-breaker, I asked the staff, 'What was the best event in your teaching last year, and why? Think for a moment.' Next I invited them to share the event with those around them. Their reticence to communicate evaporated as teachers described a feel-good event. Teachers named practical joys such as: 'I stopped using textbooks and I made learning more exciting for pupils', 'I helped others attain feelings of success and self-worth for example a child with dyscalculia wrote elaborately worded problems for the class to solve', 'when Pupil X smiled and said, I've got it'.

Next I asked, 'Why was this event so important?' I invited them to try to state the reason in one word or phrase. Each group wrote their chosen reason on a wipe-clean board. Gradually, with the help of colleagues, they teased out and named the underlying professional value that made them decide on this as a best event. For the examples above teachers named living values (Whitehead 1989) such as care (when pupil said, I've got it), respect (I helped others attain feelings of self-worth) and integrity (made learning more exciting for pupils). As a group we reviewed what we had written on the wipe-clean boards and one staff member recorded them on an interactive whiteboard, from which they were later printed and circulated. Through doing this exercise together teachers made a really exciting discovery. The values that the group had named generally correlated to teachers' professional values as identified by the Teaching Council of Ireland (2012b). (Research Diary, October 2012)

As a facilitator I learned that I could encourage active engagement in the whole-school learning community by asking participants initially to name and discuss what they personally valued as good teaching. Similar to my classroom learning community which I described in the beginning of this chapter, I found that positive experiences can motivate learning. Participants' commitment was aroused by the new experience, for them, of articulating the links between positive teaching incidents and their real or living values (Whitehead 1989). Living values affect how we act, teach and think. The participants in whole-school groups discovered how the ethical values of their profession (Teaching Council of Ireland 2016b; Glenn et al. 2012) actually affected how they acted, taught and thought (Glenn et al. 2012). By tapping into positive professional knowledge, they had articulated quality professionalism in practice. Their professional ethical values were no longer merely vague ideals or standards to be striven for but could actually be seen as existing in practice.

My initial questions hooked staff into a process of reflection within a professional community. I had intuitively chosen a positive teaching event for them to focus on, but later found that this was supported in the literature (Cooperrider et al. 2008; Kitching et al. 2009). Appreciative Inquiry works from the assumption 'that every organisation has something that works well' (Cooperrider et al. 2008: 3) and invites participants to 'share stories about their past and present achievements, assets, unexplored potentials' (ibid.). But in contrast to Appreciative Inquiry, which seeks to identify the positive core of an organization and harness this towards a change agenda, our participants identified positive achievements as a way of motivating them towards personal changes in practice. The positive achievements which our participants discussed were what Kitching et al. (2009: 43) call 'affect-triggering incidents (ATIs)'. They claim that such events, which can be either strongly positive or strongly negative, influence teacher motivation and resilience in their early careers. While I agree with these findings, I further found that naming and discussing positive ATIs enabled staff members to be motivated and become more fully engaged. At that time this was new learning for me because while teachers are generally able to identify what motivates pupils, they rarely spend time examining their own motivation. Since the time of the example above, we authors have used this strategy with many other learning communities. Our participants ranged from the newly qualified to teachers with forty plus years' experience. While Kitching's research focused on newly qualified teachers, we found our approach has implications across the continuum of professional development.

Here is a further example of how ATIs might explain these teachers' continued commitment: each learning community was invited to address questions about what each teacher and the whole-school groups believed was important in education, such as,

1.  Recall a time when you were asked to discuss the purpose of education.

2.  Do you know what the main differences might be between a teacher-centred classroom and a student- or learner-centred classroom? Which do you think would be more conducive to independent learning?

3.  Do you see knowledge as a product or a process? What do you think is the general perception of knowledge?

4.  What kind of student do you consider to be a good student? Why do you think so? Teachers commented that 'this is the first time we discussed education since initial teacher education' and some asked questions of the kind: 'Where is my voice within policy and practice?' (Research Diary, October 2012)

In this quote, the teacher reflected the idea that although many participants had previously shared the practical tips and tricks of teaching, they were now all beginning to engage critically with learning about how they taught. In whole-school learning communities, by sharing, in our own words, our understandings of changes as we experience them, can be seen as a learning history. Coghlan and Brydon-Miller (2014) say that learning history goes beyond what Roth and Kleiner (1998) called listing best practices and into the 'thinking, experimentation and arguments of those who share the same situation' (Coghlan and Brydon-Miller 2014: 493). In our learning communities we found that moving from an individual's story to the collective learning history story usually developed over three stages. First, in the make-a-start phase, participants introduced what was important to each of them in the real world of their practice. The second phase was about making connections. For example, many participants were connecting their personal teaching experiences to the bigger picture of their understandings about education. In doing so they also shared these understandings with each other. In the final phase of learning history activity, participants tried to make sense of their varying perspectives. For example, some saw that the learner-centred classroom and the teacher-centred classroom are based on two different sets of ideas about what education means. Some participants even challenged the varying views on this, such as Dewey's (1933) portrayal of education as an opportunity to learn how to apply previous experiences in new ways and Vygotsky's (1978) ideas on the scaffolding of pupil learning.

Their critiques, though practice-informed, were similar to those proposed by Prawat (2002), O'Brien (2002), and Gredler and Shields (2004) on Glassman's (2001) view that 'Dewey sees the child as a free agent who achieves goals through her own interest in the activity. Vygotsky suggests there should be greater control by a mentor who creates activity that will lead the child towards mastery' (3). The collaborative learning histories, as they were generated by the participants, became a catalyst that advanced their actions and thinking.

The benefits, for participants who contributed to a shared learning history, were both the creation of a shared identity (see Chapter 2) and the improvement practice or understanding of it. The participants' sense of ownership of their work, their autonomy and their joy gave a new positive perspective on whole-school self-evaluation as a shared endeavour. As Coghlan and Brannick (2014) put it, 'the generative insight underpinning learning history is that by capturing what groups have learned, and presenting it through the jointly-told tale, [participants] can learn about organisational change' (ibid.: xx). In our whole-school, self-evaluation communities, learning histories can be read in both the individual teacher's personal action plans and evaluations of them and in the five-part reports of whole-school meetings during the action research project.

When I facilitated my first whole-school learning community, I was impressed by how motivated the staff became. Over the years there have been many theories on motivation relevant to teaching and learning that may explain this. As far back as 1966 Atkinson and Feather speak about being motivated by the need for achievement. Yet the whole-school learning communities we supported did not have any specific achievement targets to begin with. Moving on to the achievement/goal motivation theories of Ames (1992) and Dweck (1986), we find they are closer to the approach we offered in that they speak about motivation as a process of moving actions and personal understandings forward rather than as a target-driven motivation. These theories do not reflect the intrinsic and sustainable motivation that I have witnessed in school learning communities. There, the motivation of participants grew organically and we can explain this as follows: the approach in which we have invited whole-school staffs to partake 'automatically creates a motivational climate' (Capel et al. 2009: 130). The practical strategies we use generate intrinsic motivation in the following way: participants take ownership of the topic they choose to investigate. They get constructive feedback in both the small-group and whole-school discussions. As their self-evaluation continues in a researcherly way, they take ownership of how they will attempt to change things and how they will show these changes to the learning community. Further constructive feedback from colleagues increases participants' sense of self-confidence and self-efficacy. This in turn leads them to take greater responsibility in ensuring that they evaluate their work as rigorously as possible. The increased intrinsic motivation that flows from their claim to important professional learning means that their enthusiasm and commitment are sustained. The significance of these activities, at both individual and group levels, is that participants' self-confidence and self-efficacy can contribute to a self-esteem that enables them to confidently state their experiential professional knowledge. Consequently, they may feel enabled to take more strategic roles in wider learning communities such as school–college partnerships. In the section that follows I look at the importance of the role of the individual in potentially enriching the knowledge base of their profession (Hiebert et al. 2002). The reflective questions that follow invite you to consider your personal intrinsic motivation.

## Reflective opportunity

Can you think of an amazing event in your recent practice and describe it?
What is the significance of this event for your teaching/practice?
How does it relate to key professional values in your setting?
How do these understandings relate to literature you have read?
Do you feel that you could have a role in potentially influencing education policy?

## Participants' freedom to own their professional knowledge

This section shows how I gradually came to realize that teachers in our professional learning communities benefitted from freedom similar to that afforded to the pupils in my classroom research as related at the beginning of the chapter. Basically, this was the freedom to take responsibility for one's own learning. I will now describe the process our whole-school learning communities adopted from initially embracing this freedom towards owning their professional knowledge. I will then explain the benefits of this approach over traditional forms of CPD. Following on from the session dealing with positive ATIs, here is an account of the next step of the process.

In advance of each session all participants in the learning communities received the minutes of the previous session and some possible suggestions that could be discussed at the next session. The focus of these suggestions was to aid all staff to initiate an action plan for self-evaluation of teaching and to open possibilities for supporting each other as follows:

| My values around teaching are | Hint: I am proud of ... and why? |
|---|---|
| Areas or items for improvement | Hint: What I want to improve/do better. |
| How might I possibly address them? | Hint: List possible strategies and resources |
| Select one area of teaching and learning to work | Hint: I am going to ... (name action) |
| Why was that area important to you | Hint: My values are ... and relevant policies or practices are ... |

As soon as the staff saw the personal 'I' focus in this session, they were again ready to start talking. They worked in self-selected groups. To speed up the process of sharing feedback from the groups to the entire staff, they again agreed to write a key word or sentence in response to a topic. To make all processes more open, equitable and transparent, a member of staff recorded the ideas live on an interactive whiteboard. This allowed the whole group to discuss and prioritise or clarify what was said. The whiteboard document was circulated to all after this session. Following the discussions each participant began a personal 'Action Plan for Self-Evaluation' (in writing) and completed it for the next session using the following framework:

I am interested in evaluating how I can improve ... Because (state why);
I might try ... (name possible plans and decide which is most relevant to why your topic);
I will try ... (name your plan of action and resources);
I value ...;
How I feel about the process so far? (State your honest opinion);
How I feel about what I have done?

I prompted them to add the word 'because' above as it gives opportunities to refer to policies, curriculum, school practices or theories about teaching and learning relevant to their specific context. (Research Diaries, 2010–16)

These practical strategies enabled whole-school staffs to engage in a collaborative, constructivist form of professional learning that differed significantly from traditional forms of CPD. Often professional learning is about the application of others' best practice, whether it be well-researched theory or well-tested tips and tricks of the classroom. By contrast, planning actions, using the suggested discussion questions, moved participants from their previous professional isolation model (see Chapter 4) towards a more collaborative way of working. As you can see from the example above, the learning process that we facilitated was evident in the practical questions we posed as well as in the accounts of the discussions, topics and explanations of what happened during and between each of the five sessions of the self-evaluation process.

During this process participants in our learning communities had the freedom to think creatively of possibilities about their personal practice and whole-school practices. I had chosen practical language and approaches so that they could initially focus on content and actions rather than academic language. Some of the questions opened new freedom of choice such as 'I might try, I will try, I feel ...' They had the freedom and opportunity to change their mental models. Mental models according to Senge et al. (1994) determine the details to which each of us pays attention and which in turn shape our actions. For example, Zhao (2011), in her work with learning communities in China, states that they have a mental model of competition rather than cooperation 'because of [a] long time spent working in the isolating and competitive culture' (1368). She concludes with a worthwhile suggestion for learning communities within school–college partnerships when she suggests the need for universities to 'keep the vision of collaborative practice as a genuine priority, rather than an add-on (Garmston and Wellman 1999; Leonard and Leonard 2003) and to reward collective work' (Zhao: 1368). Working mainly in Ireland, in less competitive and prescriptive contexts, we authors found that mental models change and grow from within. The process we offered whole-school learning communities supported freedom to engage with positive and personal growth mindsets (Dweck 2006).

My understanding of growth mindset is a growth stance where one wants to learn. This involves taking on challenges and working hard to confront difficulties (Dweck 2012). Dweck claims that the most motivated and resilient learners 'are the ones who believe that their abilities can be developed through their effort and learning' (2007: 6). For me, both as facilitator of, or/and participant in, learning communities, this is an important message. It is important because in encouraging the learning communities to conduct action research, I was inviting them to challenge themselves, and offering them a process to become resilient in confronting difficulties in their practice. Aronson et al. (2002), Dweck (2007) and Good et al. (2003) show that a growth mindset results in increased motivation and greater achievements. In the next section of this chapter we will examine how these can support formal evaluation of teaching and learning.

We have found that the following supported participants in more freely articulating their professional knowledge: having a personalized focus, initially using accessible/practical language, facilitating epistemologically sound forms of learning activities, and allowing participants the freedom to develop a growth mindset that is grounded in the idea that change grows from within. As facilitators of such groups, we have learned that in collaborative discussions, participants often need time to internalize feedback and incorporate it into improved learning behaviours and teaching practices. We have also found that it is necessary for each member in the learning community to be clear on what difference they want to make. This may involve forming a personal and specific research question of the kind, 'How do I improve …?' (McDonagh et al. 2012; Sullivan et al. 2016; Whitehead 1989). The reflective questions that follow invite you to consider influences and challenges in implementing change within your personal context.

# Reflective opportunity

Is it easier to change something at a practical level or to change how you think about it? Why/why not?

Who or what might influence how you think about your work as a member of a school staff?

What motivates you to stay involved in a project?

# How learning communities can support teachers in the *self-evaluation* process

The learning communities which we supported offered participants opportunities both to evaluate new personal and professional practices and also to validate new personal and professional knowledge.

## *Evaluating new personal and professional practices*

I will now explain how learning communities conducted self-evaluation of teaching and learning. Our approach was non-coercive and reflective and followed current thinking on how best to improve teaching. To 'improve teaching practice there is a need to focus on developing reflective teachers' (Government of Ireland 2015: 2). This stance, with which we agree, appears to challenge the wording 'teacher appraisal' (OECD 2013; England, Department for Education 2012), with its concentration on accountability. Evaluating effective change and supporting the development of new practices, as Hislop (2013) states, requires that 'there should be dialogue about teaching, learning and standards in schools before any consideration of evaluation or appraisal takes place' (12). He goes on to suggest that this can happen when practitioners recognize the need to reflect on their practice, contribute to conversations with their colleagues and are open to having their practice observed and discussed by colleagues (ibid.). In our learning communities, we have found that this open and reflective stance cannot be imposed but grows from within when teachers are introduced to critical reflection and critical pedagogy (Sullivan et al. 2016). Furthermore, our participants engaged in rigorous validation processes to test their claims of improvement.

There follows a description of a process that we used when supporting self-evaluation for a whole-school learning community: participants identified a concern, they named their values, they took action to improve their practice, they monitored and evaluated their actions using their values as criteria and they explored the potential significance of what they did (Whitehead and McNiff 2006). As the participants worked their way through the stages outlined above, the process was documented, and school heads retained summaries of each session as evidence of whole-staff engagement in self-evaluation of teaching. Each teacher individually wrote and retained evidence of engaging in action planning and self-evaluation. At the end of each session teachers took on homework. Here is an example of what happened when they tried to find data to show the changes they had made. This was new to them as, previously, their understanding of data was solely statistical.

> As the small group discussions began I could hear phrases like 'I couldn't believe it', 'This was all I could bring but I know ...'. There seemed to be uncertainty about what was data. So each participant reflected individually, and then in small groups, on the following questions.
>
> Has your understanding or your practice changed in any way? If so, describe what you think may be significant learning for yourself.
>
> How do you know? In other words, have you evidence of change/improvement in your understanding or in your practice?
>
> What were your criteria for judging such improvement?
>
> Again each group teased out how they might address the questions, and helped each other to identify, articulate and validate any new professional learning. (Research Diary, December 2012)

To clarify what data might look like, groups listed ways of gathering information about change and these were included in the evaluation documentation. Generally, these lists were very practical and included:

- usual professional tests – such as assessment of non-core subjects with online quizzes and projects, samples of pupils' work;

- documentation showing actions and differentiation – such as changes made to term plans or lesson plans to include pupil self-evaluation, personal reflection and differentiation, changes in lesson planning diary to include new teaching approaches or learning strategies, timetable changes, reorganization of information workfiles, new resources such as websites.

- a personal diary to show reflection on practice and reflection in practice (Schön 1995; Sullivan et al. 2016).

- personal and whole-school self-evaluation summaries from previous sessions.

## *Validity in whole-school self-evaluation*

Once participants had gathered such data, the next step was to evaluate what had happened. Those who used commercial class tests analysed the results. But these alone were not sufficient. In order to evaluate the whole-school self-evaluation themes of school leadership and management, planning, curriculum provision, teaching and learning and support for pupils (Ireland, Department of Education and Skills 2012a and 2012b; Ireland, Department of Education and Skills 2016a and 2016b), we needed to develop validation processes. We invited participants to revisit their values and assist each other as critical friends (see Chapters 1 and 2), to test if these values were evident in their practice. In addition, we offered our learning communities two research-based approaches to demonstrate the validity of any evaluations they made. These were the establishment of validation groups and the use of triangulation. To evaluate their data, each staff member presented their data to small groups of peers who had agreed to act as validation groups. We found that a learning community can readily act as a validation group. These groups questioned the accuracy and reliability of both the research approach and the practice of conducting it (Sullivan et al. 2016).

Triangulation involves examining what happened from a number of perspectives in order to establish the truthfulness of what we claim. This often means collecting verification about the same topic from different sources, for example from staff, students and parents. We also used methodological triangulation which involves choosing a variety of data-gathering tools to evaluate a topic. These could include interviews, artefacts, journals. By acting as observers, participants provided outsider observer triangulation. These observers were not directly involved in a teacher's project, but they were invited to critique what they observed. So, whole-school learning communities found valid ways to check that change had happened. Colleagues supported the evaluation of individual, and whole school, plans and actions. Their learning community evaluated the truthfulness of what participants claimed to have done. Pupils added valuable insights to the evaluation process when their experiences of learning were included. The legitimacy of each teacher's personal self-evaluation and of the whole-school self-evaluation was established though the research tools of triangulation and validation meetings.

Whole-school self-evaluation was the umbrella under which we supported the evaluation of new personal and professional practices. By enabling school staffs to evaluate their work, using a self-study action research approach, participants have claimed that 'they have felt professionally enabled and empowered, as they systematically analysed and improved their own practice' (Glenn et al. 2012: 19). Before we examine the significance of this, take some time to consider ways of supporting the evaluation of changes in practice.

# Reflective opportunity

Where might professional learning communities find data about changes in practice?

How might you document the suggestions or decisions of a validation group?

Who might you include in the triangulation of data from a whole-school perspective?

# Tapping into teachers' experiential and professional knowledge

In my classroom research at the beginning of this chapter, I described how it is necessary to respect all participants as valued experts who can make worthwhile contributions to their learning community. To conclude this chapter, I first question how teachers could be positioned as valued experts within learning communities. I then explain the potential significance of identifying and acknowledging the experiential knowledge of teachers within whole-school learning communities.

## *Participants as valued experts within whole-school learning communities*

In the activities of the whole-school learning communities, each person was encouraged to consider how they might use their professional insights into their practice to inform and improve their own work. Our choice of a self-study action research approach, enabled teachers to contribute to peer-supported and individualized teacher-centred professional development. Within our professional learning communities, the importance of the individual was recognized in that the process was

- authentic and relevant because it was informed by data from each teacher's own classroom

- collaborative and was supported by colleagues in the school community, subject co-ordinators and head teachers

- supported by facilitators who had the skills and knowledge to create practice and research-based teacher activities so that teachers felt safe yet sufficiently challenged for growth to occur.

So, each participant – facilitator and staff alike – was a valued expert in this process. There were opportunities within our whole-school learning communities for diversity, creativity and adaptability in individualized professional learning. We believe our process went beyond the pervasive discourses of the 'effective school' and more latterly the 'school improvement' movement with its drive for league tables and 'continuous school improvement' (Watson 2014: 27) by acknowledging each individual as an expert within a community of experts in their school.

## *Identifying and acknowledging the experiential knowledge of participants*

Finally, we return to the original concern of this chapter, which was the question of teachers' confidence in contributing to school–college partnerships for continuous professional learning, as acknowledged experts in teaching and learning. We have shown how our learning communities supported the participants and whole schools to tap into their experiential knowledge and to become confident in their professionalism. This confidence originated in the collaborative activities in our whole-school projects. This initially mirrored the findings of Aubussona et al. (2007) who found that action learning projects which incorporated a pedagogical framework gave participants the opportunity to gather evidence about a contextually relevant question, goal, need or problem. In addition, we found that our approach enabled grounded professional discourse that contributed to teachers' knowledge about their teaching. We also observed, in our whole-school learning communities, an increased openness and a commitment to take responsibility for the learning of others. These findings show that, in terms of a more mature professional development, 'learning happened from the bottom up rather than the usual top down' (McDonagh 2007: 210). We were making the implicit professional knowledge explicit (Day and Sachs 2004; Giovanelli 2015).

We believe that our approach to knowledge creation and learning, which we have shown to be successful in whole-school learning communities, is appropriate for all in school–college partnerships. It goes further than Beck et al. (1999) who investigated university and school partnerships from the perspective of enhancing student teachers' learning only. It also goes further than with whole-school self-evaluation where the focus is mainly on enhancing student learning (Harris and Sass 2008; OECD 2013; Rivkin et al. 2005). Such literatures suggest that while stakeholders themselves are encouraged to take on responsibility for their own learning, the process implies that stakeholders should apply others' theories about teaching and learning. We, on the other hand, promote a more holistic and empowering approach to such partnerships where everyone involved is exposed to personalized ways of learning and knowing.

# To conclude

The experiences we have discussed in this chapter show how we created a space for the fusion of continuing professional learning for both individual practising teachers and for whole-school groups. We have given schools a team approach, with reflection, evaluation and improvement built in, for tapping into the knowledge of the school community and for generating new theoretical knowledge within the school context. As we reflected on our research and on our roles as teachers, researchers and teacher educators, we summarized practical ways for sustaining the new practices developed in whole-school learning communities.

Together with my colleagues (Glenn et al. 2012 and 2012; Roche et al. 2010), we found how to encourage teachers to identify and acknowledge their good practice with confidence and to show that they are part of communities of good professional practice. In the next chapter we explore further the effects of this new epistemology on participants and facilitators of learning communities.

# 8

# What's in This for Me? From the Perspective of Participating Teachers, Teacher Educators and Leaders

*Caitriona McDonagh*

## Introduction

This chapter is about the transformative effects of learning communities. Teachers tell what they learned from participating in the range of learning communities that we supported, and teacher educators and leaders of such groups tell of their learning. Over the period 2008 to 2016, these learning communities included all sectors of education; whole-school staffs; inter-school subject groups; networks; face-to-face, online and blended courses. During this time, we worked with four national universities and three private third-level colleges.

In the first part of this chapter we look at what teachers and practitioners said they gained from taking part in learning communities. They claimed that one of the benefits of engaging in these professional conversations with colleagues was that it contributed to a greater confidence in taking more powerful positions in the fields of both initial teacher education (as more equal partners in school–college partnerships) and continuing professional development, as well as in school policymaking. Part of this confidence-building process was the significance for teachers of their new insights into their practice, as detailed in the previous chapter. We examine how teachers developed evidence of improvements in teaching and learning and also hear of some of the challenges they faced within these communities. The second part of this chapter looks at our learning experiences as facilitators of a variety of learning communities. As facilitators, we authors wear many hats in that we have also been teacher educators, school leaders, curricular subject coordinators and have also held leadership roles for coordinating teaching and learning in schools during the course of the events documented in this book. We came to understand the significance of collaborative self-evaluation and of using a self-study action research approach in empowering teachers to build on their professional strengths. We have now become more convinced of the viability of our approach as a sustainable way of researching and improving practice across sectors.

In this chapter I explore:

- teachers' explanations of how they
  - ➤ benefitted from becoming more critically reflective
  - ➤ generated new knowledge and generated theory about teaching and learning
  - ➤ attempted to contribute to the knowledge base of the profession.
- teacher educators' and leaders' explanations of
  - ➤ the challenges and benefits of an open, vibrant, non-coercive approach
  - ➤ the importance of the strengths-based approach
  - ➤ the power of a differentiated rather than a summative process.

# What's in this for me: participating teachers explain

In earlier chapters you have heard how participants learned from their experiences in our communities where action research became the glue that helped them to take charge of making the changes that they deemed necessary in their practice. In Chapters 3 and 4 participants claimed to have experienced a valid form of CPD that enabled them to become more inclusive and democratic in their classrooms and to experience learning communities as models for classroom interactions. In Chapters 5 and 6, participants claimed that they recognized themselves as extended professionals who reflected on a much wider vision of what education involves, and valued the theory underpinning pedagogy, and where student teachers recognized themselves as knowers. In Chapter 7 teachers told how they could feel confident in their professionalism by systematically examining their practice, evaluating teaching and learning and taking responsibility for their own learning.

In this chapter you will hear in the participants' own words an account of the three most transformative aspects of the educational learning communities we supported, which they named as controlling their professional learning, generating new knowledge and theory about teaching and learning and contributing to the knowledge base of their profession. Some comments were encouraging, such as: 'I found it quite therapeutic' and 'It has re-ignited my love of teaching after a hard year in the classroom' (Evaluations 2013). But at times participants described how some events were challenging, and we offer our explanations which may guide others on their journey to participating in and/or supporting similar learning communities. Our explanations are based on analyses of all the learning communities we supported between 2008 and 2016, and incorporate the Teaching Council of Ireland Practice-Based Research Project (Glenn et al. 2012) as well as whole-school learning communities during the years that followed. We analysed teacher feedback in relation to working together, as they collaboratively researched both personal and whole-group areas of interest, using an action research methodology. The examples in this chapter show that our action research approach allowed teachers' interactions and connections in learning communities to become more critically reflective and 'wholly oriented towards learners, through a transformational shift in relationships' (Somekh and Noffke 2009: 522).

## Teachers benefitting from being more critically reflective

Teachers told how continuous professional learning was at its best when it shifted from them passively listening to lectures and exemplars to engaging in critically reflective and researcherly practice within our learning communities as described in this book. As teachers took more control of their professional learning, opportunities arose for them to get on the inside of ideas and establish a critically reflective practice. The example below is from one such community where all the teachers were supporting pupils with special education needs. Here a teacher describes how she learned to become more reflective and critical within this inter-school subject group.

We discussed educational provision for pupils with special educational needs. We shared ideas and advised each other on how to deal with specific needs of pupils. Having four brains instead of one was so beneficial! The four of us had different strengths, personalities and outlooks on teaching so we pushed each other to view things in a different way. To be able to get an outside opinion really guided me and helped me provide the best education that I could for my pupils. I feel I grew on a personal level by sharing my experiences. Often my work is in isolation. I would love to become more collaborative with professional colleagues in future. Our learning circle minimised stress levels. The group dynamics were affirming, as we were trying to satisfy both our intellectual and practical curiosity. We all shared our opinions and came away from each session feeling positive and having benefitted from the opinions of others. At times we became mentors to each other and sent each other little motivating texts during the week. Teachers need mentors (O'Doherty and Deegan 2009). One member of the group is familiar with working in other countries and loved quoting research – something I did not do, except when it was required on accredited courses. Previously research seemed to have little relevance to me as it seemed to be generally large scale reports. As I got deeper into this learning community and action research, I have changed. I have begun to plan for gaps in my pupils learning (Stiggins 2004) to improve my assessment for learning (Earle 2014), for example 'yard' (supervision of pupils' free play time during school hours) is a time when I can learn so much about pupils – I never knew that before. A lot of my observation notes are now based on children's interactions with each other. I learned that getting pupils to transfer knowledge, not only from one task to another but also to other skills, is important for our pupils with additional needs. (Learning Circle, November 2014)

This teacher described two important aspects of learning communities for her. (i) She had the freedom and opportunity to delve into areas of particular interest to her. (ii) The ideas of others in the group and her interactions with other participants changed many of her perceptions and practices. In the example above, and in other learning communities with which we worked, many teachers appreciated the freedom to delve into understanding particular areas of practice, and emphasized the importance for them of having opportunities to reflect on their work, and to collaborate in making sense of their world. Teachers found a process that excited their professional curiosity and encouraged fluid and developmental thinking regardless of where they were in their careers. Through reflection they became more aware of themselves as persons. They realized the wide variety of influences on their professional knowledge, such as pupils, other practice experts, other educationalists and literatures from the fields of social sciences, psychology, knowledge transfer, management of learning, research and policy, among others. They claimed to have become more critically aware, which informed and transformed how they thought and taught (Sullivan et al. 2016).

The second transformative aspect described by the teacher in the example above grew from the complexity of teacher interactions within the learning community. The importance of such interactions is rarely addressed in the provision of CPD. Yet teachers' perspectives on the most effective types of CPD show a preference for face-to-face, school-based professional discussions, engaging in informal dialogue that is followed by peer observation and mentoring (Walsh 2016). In addition, the quantitative study by Weissenrieder et al. (2015) links teachers' self-efficacy to collaboration in professional learning communities. In the examples below, teachers talk about these links plus the additional unanticipated professional effects of fostering collegial interactions. These interactions provided openings for them to think critically about what influenced them as they investigated their teaching and learning. Similar to the teachers in our groups, Sjoer and Meirink (2016) found that teachers can exchange many practice skills and are able to synthesize ideas from practice. In their studies of similar joint school-based learning communities, they also found that teachers could 'formulate and develop a shared vision and curriculum' (Sjoer and Meirink 2016: 110). But the transformative difference that participants said they experienced in our learning communities was instigated by how we supported critical thinking in teaching and learning, rather than aiming for consensus in curricular areas (see 'School Two' at the beginning of Chapter 7).

Our analysis of what teachers said shows that we went beyond the literatures above. At a practice level, teachers expressed surprise that they had not engaged in such critically reflective dialogue prior to our programme and spoke of its benefits as follows: 'It helped me to focus more', 'I never even thought about these things before!' 'It was great to be able to bring something to the table and get feedback on it' and 'It was fascinating to hear other people's interests and try out their ideas' (Feedback, November 2011). Participants stated that they had never undertaken CPD to deepen their understanding of their practice but now that they had tried it, they were hooked. One participant commented: 'I felt very much part of a group and took energy and joy from the group. We all celebrated each other's successes however small, and I think this gave us the courage to persevere in our endeavours' (Feedback, December 2012).

Empowerment through professional dialogue was key according to those teachers who had a role in school leadership. For example, one said, 'It's great to see the staff interacting on a professional level – sharing expertise, learning how to improve teaching and learning' (Validation meeting, January 2012). A school head commented that the biggest change she could see was the increased level of communication in the school: 'The participants here learned whole new methodologies for teaching, improving administration, pedagogy and curriculum through their dialogue with one another and they blossomed in the sharing process' (Validation meeting, July 2011).

The teacher evaluations also illuminate some of the problematics in the ongoing debates on how to evaluate CPD despite the wide variety of designers and providers of CPD programmes (Earley and Porritt 2010; King 2014; OFSTED 2006; Teaching Council of Ireland 2016). We believe that our learning communities and the testimony above show viable and valid outcomes for sustainable professional learning. Some hold that effective CPD is a 'growth of teacher expertise that leads to a change in practices resulting in improved practices, and in improved student learning' (AITSL 2014: 19). Participating teachers in our learning communities stated that they achieved this. They further maintained that they had become self-directed agents taking responsibility for their own professional growth (Day and Sachs 2004). Consequently, their professional development was sustainable since it is an integral part of their professional life, or as Barak et al. (2010: 275) describe it, 'a fertile ground for sustainable change and development'. This finding mirrors our personal experience of conducting self-study action research as part of a learning community, as explained in Chapters 1 and 2. We believe that teachers' claims of self-efficacy have grown from the opportunities to become more critically reflective, and from the interactions within our learning communities.

## Teachers generated new knowledge and theory about teaching and learning

In this section, participating teachers within a variety of learning communities tell how they came to make a claim of new learning for themselves where they had gained expertise from reflecting on their teaching and taking action to try to improve things. Some participants were working towards academic accreditation. Others were researching issues such as school self-evaluation, school improvement or enhancing teaching for the benefit of their students. Regardless of their reasons for getting involved, participants in our learning communities were supported to become theorists by developing living theories from within their daily practice. In order to theorize their practice, teachers needed to present evidence of change or improvement. A learning community can be supportive in this demanding process of demonstrating reliability, credibility and validity in the research (Sullivan et al. 2016). Teachers told how they worked through five key steps in order to establish a credible claim to new knowledge (or a personal theory). These steps were (1) making a claim to new knowledge or learning, (2) showing evidence of your claim, (3) using your values as criteria on which your claim can be judged, (4) testing your claim against those criteria, and (5) disseminating your findings and your personal theories. We will examine each in turn from the teachers' perspectives.

**1.** Making a claim to new knowledge or learning

Participants initially found it difficult to word a claim to new knowledge or theory. This may be because professional knowledge is generally identified by outsiders assessing teachers' competencies rather than by teachers naming their personal attainments. So the challenge of how to word a claim to new knowledge needed to be addressed and here is how a participating school head described his process.

> I maintained an open door policy. But every day I felt frustrated because of the challenge of communicating all school notices to a large staff while also having time to deal with critical personal issues that arose for individual staff members. I was frustrated because although, I believed in fairness and equality, these qualities were not always evident in my daily work. My research plan and actions were to make an announcement daily at 10am of all public notices and to pull down the blind on my office door when dealing with private issues of staff. Both actions could be verified by staff. A critical friend confirmed the evidence in my journal showing that my frustration had lessened. Anecdotal data from staff could also be included but I now know that these are not evidence until validated. My claim was 'I have developed a more equitable and fair theory of practice for communicating with staff members at a personal and at a whole staff level.' The wording of my claim included my values of equality and fairness. My initial open door policy displayed these values. My frustrations were that I was not showing these. I was not living to these values in that I was not fair to myself and was concerned about dealing with all staff members equally. The wording of my personal theory also included a claim of change in practice. I found my professional learning group very helpful in teasing out the wording I chose. (Research Journal, June 2012)

**2.** Showing evidence of a claim

As in the example above, participants, with the support of colleagues in a learning community, found that they could readily describe improvement in their practice or their understanding of it. Many made lists of data that could show improvements or changes in their practice.

**3.** Using values as criteria for judging a claim

Many participants said that this was a most challenging aspect. Initially, they often felt that in order to show improvement in their practice they needed to do a pre- and post-test of student learning. Their perspectives can be explained by current thinking and practice where education contexts are generally externally driven by accountability matrices which value numerical demonstrations of improvement, as in league tables of schools. Some teachers even felt their practices were only evaluated by a summative assessment of student learning, generally carried out in a written terminal exam format. As teachers' thinking developed within our learning communities, they realized that 'this alone cannot demonstrate evidence of improvement in my teaching' (Participant Evaluations, 2012). They also came to appreciate that 'there is a need to focus on self-change and to provide criteria that could be used to assess such changes' (ibid.). These criteria are closely aligned to the *values* held by the practitioner. In the example above, the head teacher chose equality and fairness as criteria for his project and many participants followed this pattern of citing strongly held professional values, as they began to test their claims that they had improved.

**4.** Testing a claim against those criteria

In some forms of research, a post-test is often used to show statistical evidence of a change in a situation. However, in educational action research, evidence of change is shown, not by statistical measurements only but also by criteria that originate in the value base of the researcher. Once teachers had selected these criteria they had less difficulty finding evidence to support their claims. A case in point is the head teacher in the example above, who said, 'both actions could be verified by staff'. Additional verification came from the triangulation of data from a variety of perspectives. For example, his reflective journal, the perspectives of colleagues and critical friends, all provided evidence of his demonstration of equality and fairness in his practice. So when he claimed: 'I have developed a more equitable and fair theory of practice for communicating with staff members at a personal and at a whole staff level', he had verification from staff that they had witnessed him acting in a more equitable and fair manner according to his values. Their confirmation demonstrates that his claim is honest and accurate. He, like other participants, demonstrated further accountability and credibility by sharing his claim publicly.

**5.** Disseminating your findings and your personal theories

Learning communities readily offered opportunities for participants to go public with their new learning. As they presented an evidence-based claim to their learning community for critical evaluation, their peers not only identified the reliability and credibility of the claim but also often recognized the significance of the research projects more readily than did the presenters. Teachers were also surprised at the variety of opportunities for presenting their new learning about practice. Although peer-reviewed journals, conferences and posters were available to those participants doing accredited research, others found ways to disseminate their new learning through teach-meets, research-meets and professional groups – subject-based or peer-to-peer groups, school-to-school partnerships or school–college partnerships. Many of those from our learning communities claimed that having their new learning commented on by colleagues was empowering. Our learning communities offered teachers opportunities to acknowledge professional expertise, and to support each other in theorizing their practice, so that they were more confident in sharing their knowledge and experiences. This often led to some revelations: in one school, for example, a staff member had designed and presented curriculum-based professional development initiatives at a national level, others had published textbooks for students, yet their work colleagues had been unaware of this.

# Teachers contributed to the knowledge base of the profession

Teachers working in our learning communities made important professional contributions in two specific ways, which we will explain:

1. They took control of their professional learning,

2. Their awareness of experiential professional knowledge and their confidence in proclaiming it had significance for the profession and for policy.

## *An explanation of how teachers took control of their professional learning*

An important aspect of inviting learning communities to undertake evaluation of their practice was that participants were offered a personalized form of professional development. This approach is about taking control of what is important in real-life teaching such as abstracting knowledge from experience. The changes recorded by teachers in our learning communities reflected attribution theory (Ganzach 2016; Weiner 1985; Wolters et al. 2013) which suggests that our achievements can be attributed or dictated by who or what is in control of our learning. Teachers told us that they took control of their professional learning, and perhaps this could explain their sustained motivation and dedication to rigorous self-evaluation as described in Chapter 7. Similarly, we can explain that effective CPD occurs when professionals answer the following questions: (a) Who is in control of my professionalism, teaching and learning? (b) Is it me (internal) or someone or something else (external)? In the following example, teachers worded their understanding of how a shift in locus of control affected the success of their learning.

> In our school self-evaluation, we freely questioned how we were dealing with the issues of interest to us. As we discussed them in our small group we either praised them or found ways to improve. The events and successes were our real daily workplace experiences. This was unlike traditional professional development where the input, and what we were expected to do about it, were controlled by something external. (Reflective Journal, June 2012)

The documentation showed that there was self-determination of goals and self-regulation of actions happening. The participants were intrinsically motivated. This could be seen in their spontaneity, creativeness and willingness to examine every aspect of the work setting that was relevant to their initial question. Their behaviours might reflect the self-determination theory (Ryan and Deci 2000) which specifies that social settings promote intrinsic motivation when they satisfy the innate psychological needs of autonomy and relatedness. Learning community members had competence in many skills which enabled them to manipulate the environment and the ways in which they worked. They had autonomy in deciding what to do and how to do it. Relatedness is seen in their interactions and professional conversations.

## *The significance of developing awareness of teacher experiential professional knowledge*

Teachers' awareness of their experiential professional knowledge and their confidence in proclaiming it has significance for the profession and for policy. Professional knowledge of teachers is not easy to quantify. When teachers participating in our learning communities were evaluating their school, or their teaching, we authors became aware of the wide spectrum of knowledge that we needed to examine in order to validate their new learning. This spectrum was evident in the diversity of topics teachers chose to investigate, and the professional insights they gained. The activities of the participating teachers had an impact on their professional qualities, skills and knowledge base, and was referenced in their evaluation of the processes we facilitated. The teachers' responses below show important links to both professional values and skills as well as to an understanding of pertinent professional knowledge:

| Professional values and relationships | teachers said, | 'It gave me opportunities to think about myself as a teacher.' |
|---|---|---|
| Professional integrity | teachers said, | 'It enabled me to more honestly evaluate my teaching and me as a teacher.' |
| Professional conduct | teachers said | 'It has changed the way I approached things.' |
| Professional practice | teachers said | 'In our group there were many examples about changes in curriculum, assessment and teaching methodologies.' |
| Professional development | teachers said | 'I question myself more and ask how I can improve and why I should try the approaches I choose.' |
| Collegiality and collaboration | teachers said | 'Having discussions makes it easier to approach colleagues: discussion with peers is beneficial.' |

(Glenn et al. 2012)

These professional qualities, skills and knowledge contributed to a 'powerful conceptual knowledge among teachers at the same time as developing teachers' knowledge for teaching and teaching practices' (Brodie 2013: 15). The action research approach (Sullivan et al. 2016) that we adopted in learning communities was a further contributory factor. Tacit knowledge includes the skills, ideas and experiences that people have, which can be difficult to access because they are often not codified and may not necessarily be easily expressed (Brock 2015; Wong 2008). This kind of knowledge can often only be revealed through practice in a particular context and transmitted through social interactions. It is an added bonus when one is able to identify this form of knowledge in a professional learning community.

# Reflective opportunity

How might I demonstrate my experiential knowledge?
How could I make a claim to improvement in teaching?
How might I show evidence of the claims I make?

# What's in this for me? Teacher educators' and leaders' explanations

In the first three sections of this chapter, teachers have named and explained what they gained from their experiences within our learning communities. Facilitators of these learning communities also claimed that they had learned from their experiences. My personal learning began with finding ways to facilitate openness and motivation. I learned that participants' motivation could be sustained by developing ways to address participants' personal and professional needs. I felt part of establishing a grass-roots or bottom-up approach to professional learning (Glenn et al. 2012) and it was one of the most invigorating educational happenings that I have ever experienced.

Facilitators can experience challenges when convening learning communities, however. Some find difficulties in moving discussion beyond cordiality, to 'navigating the fault lines' of divergent views and 'negotiating the essential tensions' (Owen 2014: 74). This is not only a challenge for facilitators but also for all group members. Working through these tensions in a researcherly way significantly benefitted the well-being and professional growth of all as I will explain later in this chapter. Sometimes things went wrong and the groups I led did not always work collaboratively. Here is an example of how I dealt with this dilemma. I began by reflecting on myself, my concern and what I could do about it. I looked at (a) my thinking, (b) my actions and (c) my influence in the group as in the reflective questions below:

a. Reflecting on myself: I asked, did I advise, assume and judge? Here are some phrases I found myself using: 'I would like to focus on what is going on between us here ...' This was helpful when there was a difference of opinion because rather than asking participants to explain their stance, I focused on the process. I also used 'I' statements rather than 'you' statements. For example, 'I think maybe ...' rather than 'you should'.

b. Reflecting on my actions: For example, when a participant started shuffling I often rushed to deliver the next piece of content, rather than asking how I could help. I found myself asking, 'Are emotions being acted out rather than being communicated?'

c. Reflecting on my influence on the group: I asked, 'Did I manipulate rather than communicate? Was I defensive or did I sound defensive? Did I preach or speak "at" people?'

Now I will consider the claims to learning that we, as facilitators, made in earlier chapters. In Chapter 1 we learned about key elements of dialogue, the single most important ingredient in our learning communities. We showed how, with action research as a catalyst, these aspects of dialogue could enhance professional identity and practice. In Chapters 3 and 4, we learned to bridge the gap between academic and practitioner knowledge. We learned more about the epistemological, ontological and methodological principles of self-study action research as we worked with both teachers and student teachers. We experienced the seamless way participants were now able to speak about philosophers, theories and practice as they explained the values base of their study in Chapters 5 and 6. In Chapter 7, we learned how to encourage intrinsic motivation and how to promote a more holistic and empowering approach for whole-school learning communities by supporting personalized ways of learning and knowing.

We are now moving on to discuss three key transformative outcomes: *the benefits of an open, vibrant, non-coercive approach; the importance of the strengths-based approach; the power of a differentiated rather than a summative process.*

# The benefits of an open vibrant, non-coercive approach according to teacher educators and leaders

Facilitators found that learning communities were most successful when they were invitational and non-coercive. An example of this invitational approach was our establishment of a network (NEARI) to address what we believed was a lack of academic nourishment for practitioners who are action researchers. The broad spectrum of action researchers that actually attended network meetings attested to the rationale for a non-coercive approach to learning communities.

We describe the importance of an open invitation and non-coercive approach in the account below. The initial invitation, from us four authors and Pip Ferguson, was emailed to all active action researchers known to the conveners of the NEARI group and we continue to use the same wording for invitations to all our events: 'Please feel free to share this advert with anyone you know who may be interested in any aspect of action research, reflective practice, critical reflection and/or improving practice' (NEARI n.p.). The inaugural meeting was interactive and the sharing brought an energy and synergy to the room. We conveners later commented on the diversity created by this invitational approach as follows:

We were a really eclectic group. Despite many people not knowing each other, there was a frank and open, and often humorous, exchanges of work/life stories and, in some cases, evidence of a real hunger for what we called 'professional nourishment'. There were people who wanted to create a site of resistance to the watering down of educational values; people who wanted to restore professional autonomy to teachers; people who didn't want to stop teaching and learning and engaging in education discourse just because they're retired; those who struggled to see the relevance of their PhD research question; some who were relieved to see that the affective domain matters in education as much as the cognitive, and that feelings were important in reflective practice. And we had some who came along with questions and went home with a whole lot of new ones. Common to many of those categories was, perhaps, the wish to be/ become/remain critical thinkers/pedagogues. (NEARI Archive, May 2015)

The open invitational approach we adopted was challenging at times for facilitators: discussions could sometimes head off in unexpected directions or could take a long time to get off the ground. Recalling that group members are those 'most affected' by decisions about teaching and learning and yet they are the 'least consulted' (Kooy 2015: 187), we anticipated outpourings. We also questioned what was happening for those who stayed on the periphery of the group. Here is how one facilitator described her experience:

Because of the diversity in the group, because of people's different geographical location and time commitments, we've needed to learn that there are some who prefer to remain somewhat peripheral. Peripheral participation was described by Lave and Wenger (1991) and also by Illeris (2002) as a situation where newcomers to a community of practice start at the periphery, and gradually, through participation in the community's activities, become inducted into the ways of the community. They may well move from the periphery to a more central position, as some of our members have done. However, there are always some who choose to remain on the periphery. They express interest in the community and its activities, but do not necessarily want to become more actively involved. We learned to value such participation and the fact that people choose to maintain links, however tenuous, without seeing it as 'failure' if the same faces do not show up to each 'live' event. (Convener Evaluation, August 2016)

As we tried to understand this concept of valuing peripheral participation, we realized that it was rooted in understandings of how learning happens and its epistemological links. Learning communities are widely used to capture tacit knowledge that is not easily documented or to increase organizational performance. This presumes that learning happens through constructivist methods, as participants help each other to move forward. This further implies that such communities offer a process for sharing knowledge. In the professional learning communities that we facilitated, knowledge was not only being shared but new knowledge was also being created, as we discussed in earlier chapters. To explain this creation of new personal knowledge I return to Polanyi's (1958) understanding of how we come to know – he stated, 'Into every act of knowing there enters a tacit and passionate contribution of the person knowing what is being known and this coefficient is no mere imperfection, but a necessary component of all knowledge' (312). Taking his words 'tacit and passionate', I think about a participant who might appear passive on the periphery, or unengaged in a group as he thinks through his new ideas or theories. His demeanour could lead to the outward appearance of withdrawal from the debates, discussion and actions of his group as he unobtrusively creates new learning for himself. Therefore, we should not dismiss those who remain on the periphery of a learning community. Using this logic, we have discovered strengths in those who chose to work at the edges of the community

## The importance of the strengths-based approach

We found that we had developed a strengths-based approach to professional learning rather than a remedial approach. Frequently action research projects begin by asking researchers to focus on what could be perceived as a negative aspect of their practice that needs improvement. Yet in our learning communities we began the research process by asking participants to identify a positive event in their practice. As a facilitator I learned that positive psychology and theories of well-being can help explain how we supported each other's critical reflection and action. Like Seligman (2003: 13), I believe that 'the highest success in living and the deepest emotional satisfaction comes from building and using your signature strengths'. Positive psychology asks questions such as 'What works?' rather than 'What doesn't?' or 'What is right with this person?' rather than 'What is wrong?' (Boniwell 2012: 5). While participants worked through such questions as: 'What are my concerns and why?', as facilitators we realized that by using a strengths-based approach in our learning communities with adults, we were not about remediation – filling holes in participants' knowledge or removing weaknesses – but we were about encouraging a community 'to identify, use and develop their strengths' (Norris and Seligman 2015: 96). These strengths included the values they held about education and how to use them as criteria in showing the validity of their research.

The following example from Chapter 4 shows what this looked like in our learning community. The facilitator told how the other members of the group enabled a post-primary teacher of mathematics to move from a curriculum- and state-examination-focused approach to a more student-centred approach with a strong emphasis on students' understanding of mathematical concepts. Coming from a primary level of teaching and from special education settings, the other participants shared their strengths in methodologies and learning strategies with the maths teacher. The individual strengths of group members, in terms of professional expertise and/or personal insights, fuelled the strengths-based approach the facilitator encouraged. In Chapter 7 there was a further example of our strengths-based approach when the facilitator invited discussions on positive affect-triggering incidents (ATIs). This was shown to contribute to the participants' motivation to engage in a learning community and also to sustain a keenness to continue critically questioning their practice.

We believe that we are creating a new critical pedagogy for facilitating learning communities. It involves giving participants opportunities to identify and appreciate their intrinsic worth and to help 'them find the niche where they can live their positive traits to the fullest' (Seligman 2003: 28) through an invitational process of personal and collaborative learning. We have found that facilitators and participants alike flourish in our learning communities when we become familiar with, and mindfully apply, our strengths to our work. This can become contagious within the community. In school communities, Fox Eades (2008) found that when teachers flourish, their students are more likely to flourish and to reach their potential too. We now understand that the recognition of one's signature strengths is a vital part of becoming a mindful and reflective teacher. We have found that this approach can contribute to mindful nurturing, well-being and happiness in one's profession.

Participating teachers claimed that the positive emotions they experienced were not only about solving immediate workplace problems, but also were about solving problems associated with personal development and growth. Fredrickson (2015) speaks of two types of positive emotions. The first type is about survival only, while the second type reflects the broadening mindset, actions and social resources which participants claimed. This broadening allows us to build up the intellectual, physical, social and psychological reserves upon which we can draw when an opportunity presents itself. So providing opportunities for participants to experience positive emotions contributes to and nurtures a sense of well-being.

We facilitators also experienced a sense of positivity as we witnessed growing degrees of participation and expertise. We became optimistic about the future of education in participants' hands and we saw that relationships within the community were a key feature. Likewise, for us as conveners and facilitators, being connected to each other as colleagues and friends gave us a sense of well-being. Our connectedness to the social network of each of the learning communities we supported, and particularly to the Network of Educational Action Research Ireland (NEARI), added to it. Yet this was not a utopian scenario. We have each individually made mistakes, and our participants also gained from their opportunities to make mistakes. We all learned from them and developed resilience. Positive psychology has been defined as the scientific study of optimal human functioning (Seligman and Csikszentmihalyi 2000). Our increasing recognition and confidence that effective learning took place in our learning communities contributes to our contentment and enjoyment of the process. Research has also shown that focusing on strengths and positive experiences, as we believe we have done, can reduce problems and prevent anxiety (Seligman et al. 2009).

# The power of a differentiated rather than a summative process

This leads nicely to the evaluation of how professional learning happened within the communities. As facilitators, we have identified differentiated rather than summative professional development as a key feature when supporting learning communities. Summative professional development can be explained as a programme where aims and learning objectives are clearly stated in advance. The evaluation of the programme depends on how the participants measure up against these previously decided learning objectives. A differentiated approach, on the other hand, is about focusing on participants as individuals with their personal strengths and learning needs. The success of a differentiated programme can be seen in how each individual participant has been enabled to learn from the process in ways that were appropriate for them. As you have seen throughout this book, the evaluation of what has been achieved in our learning communities is not presented in charts and tables but in what individual participants and facilitators have been able to show as their personal new learning.

We structured programmes around the pace of development in participants' thinking. This has particular significance when communities come together with the aim of organizational change. We facilitators now know the necessity for an individual research project as well as a group research element. The following example gives a sense of what this looked like in practice and why it is so important. Here, a teacher explains the impact of a learning community on her thinking:

> Reflection, which is an important component of action research, begins with self but our learning impacts on self and others, namely our pupils and colleagues. The difficulty is how to translate collaboration into action. Collaboration that stops at discussion only is not going to feed into practice. A structure and an action plan are required. The programme helped me realise that change is difficult, but possible. We may know how to teach but as teachers we need to develop our understanding and knowledge. These are fundamental to change and will thrive in a well-developed community of practice as explained by Fullan (1993) and Wenger (1998). My school has decided to examine literacy. There is a danger of becoming over-reliant on standardised tests to assess learning. The programme has prompted me to raise this issue in school and to examine other ways to explore assessment for learning from the publication *Assessment in Primary Schools* (NCCA 2007). I am researching a co-operative learning resource for comprehension with a view to its implementation through collaboration between the Learning Support team and class teachers in school. I keep a reflective journal to record the positive and negative aspects of my practice. I get pupils' views on the various roles they experience in using a cooperative learning strategy. I get colleagues' evaluations on our learning and on the pupils' learning. (Online Course Evaluations, September 2013)

Phrases such as 'begins with the self', 'change is difficult', 'translate collaboration', 'raise issues' and 'assessment for learning' prompted facilitators to realize that learning is not something that is done to organizations, nor is it something that an organization does. This gave rise to the understanding that learning and organizing are seen as 'mutually constitutive and unstable, yet pragmatic, constructs that might enable a dynamic appreciation of organisational life' (Clegg et al. 2005: 150). We facilitators discovered that indeed participants gained an appreciation and much greater understanding both of their own practice and the organizations in which they worked. This was in part due to the critical reflection stance we encouraged. Here is how one facilitator described their learning.

> We facilitators had an enthusiasm and commitment to learning communities of action researchers, but we accept that such communities are not for everyone. Our approach was particularly suited to those who want to experience the excitement of learning. It is for those who are, or who are

willing to become critical thinkers. As facilitators we realised that there are many paths to knowledge which participants in learning communities can travel to nourish their critical thinking. (NEARI Archive, May 2015)

To summarize what conveners have learned: the success of professional learning communities depends on sustained critical reflection among their participants, including the leaders. This can be inhibited in many ways such as when leaders are too directive, inflexible, format driven, or where practice is emphasized at the expense of theories and supporting critical thinking (Hargreaves 2013; Sullivan et al. 2016). Some leaders say that it is enough to be in the role of an attentive observer, trying to spot, act, improve and find the next step in learning activities for the group. Other leaders say that participants learn as if they did not exist. This mirrors Montessori (1949: 404) who points out that 'the best sign of success is when the teacher can say, "The children are now working as if I did not exist" '.

## Reflective opportunity

Think about when you have facilitated new learning for a group.

If you altered your approach for any reason, can you say what you learned from this change?
How did you evaluate your effectiveness as a convener/facilitator?
What data might you gather to show this?
How did you judge participants' reactions to your approach?

## To conclude

This chapter has focused on learning and professional nourishment from the perspective of teachers and facilitators alike. As Apte (2009) says, 'Learning is about transformation, it's about change, it's about seeing yourself in relation to the world differently' (168). We, conveners of learning communities, have come to understand the power of how teachers work together to create a sustainable form of transformation.

Since we embarked on our journey of convening learning communities, we have learned to help groups move from practice issues to developing an understanding of many aspects of teaching. The collaborative and critically reflective culture we have encouraged and our effective learning activities enabled change in practice and in belief. Teachers have said that belief in their professionalism was a catalyst for critical reflection, and the generation of new knowledge and theory about teaching and learning could contribute to the knowledge base of the profession.

As conveners of learning communities, we authors have found that in union with members of our learning communities, we too feel sustained, validated, reinforced and rejuvenated in our work.

# Conclusion

This is the end of our book but not the end of our learning journey. As we write this conclusion we hope that our endeavour has guided readers towards understanding a new educational framework for developing their own learning communities, where a critical and questioning disposition can be nurtured. In the real-life experiences that we have described, and in the explanations of them, readers have heard how participants engaged in a variety of processes of enquiry within learning communities, and how this enabled them to have an educational influence in their own learning and in the learning of others (Carr and Kemmis 1986; Kincheloe 2003; McNiff and Whitehead 2005; Sullivan et al. 2016; Whitehead 2015). We authors espouse the principle of contributive social justice (McDonagh 2007) where participants engage on an equal footing with one another. The prerequisites for this principle are: first, providing the freedom for the individual to gain confidence in his or her own abilities; and second, providing the freedom for critical reflection and action.

Our learning communities were innovative because they embraced both theory and practice. We feel that we cannot discuss theory and practice as separate entities, because there is a constant interplay between them. Our research has always been about crossing boundaries and we believe we have shown how we regularly cross the theory–practice divide in the various learning communities we convened and in which we participated. Our book is a narrative of the creation of spaces which set out to nurture experiential knowledge and theory generation, building on existing teaching and learning expertise and collaborative critical reflection. The experiences that we discussed throughout the book show how we contributed to the creation of new hybrid spaces for continuing professional learning, for ourselves, for individual practising teachers, for whole-school groups and for student teachers. Many of the teachers who participated in our professional learning programmes and courses have begun the process of systematically examining their practice and implementing changes leading to improvement, and have now developed new knowledge about their practice or their understanding of it. When teachers become self-directed agents taking responsibility for their own professional growth (Day and Sachs 2004), they feel more empowered and professional development consequently becomes an integral part of professional life (Barak et al. 2010).

We began with the story of our own engagement in a learning community: we explained how we were amazed by the quality of our learning and the power of belonging to such a community. We sought to extend this excitement by sharing it with others and we convened new learning communities for the following: groups of teachers meeting together outside school time; whole-school groups meeting during and after school hours; student teachers in an ITE context and school–college partners. We also started online in-service programmes for teachers. We developed our living educational theory (Whitehead 1989) of learning communities as each participant developed their understanding of their practice. We lived towards our values around knowledge creation: we did not act as experts within our learning communities. Instead, each individual teacher created and articulated their own new learning. We believe that this approach demonstrates a new topology of theory–practice where each participant has an equal status as theory generator and practitioner. In such a landscape there is no space for hierarchy, posturing or power-wielding. Each participant has something to offer: this contrasts, as we said earlier, with the deficit model of professional development which is grounded in a separation of expert knowers and learners. Instead, drawing on Buber's (1958) I–Thou approach, we argue that all participants can recognize the potential for knowledge creation in the other, in a merging of ontological, epistemological and methodological values.

In this book we have presented our basic ideas and we invite people to utilize them, tweak them and move them forward if they wish. In a reciprocal spirit of sharing and collaborating, we hope that our readers have enjoyed accompanying us on our journey of exploration and self-discovery, and are now enticed to experience for themselves the life-enhancing benefits of engaging in self-study action research in a learning community. The approach we have taken here may be challenging and we acknowledge that each group must create the community that best suits their situation. Paraphrasing Etienne Wenger-Trayner (foreword), we are not offering a template or a 'top-down mandate': rather, we are inviting you, having reflected on our book, to reveal your passion and your enthusiasm for learning together, for your own benefit and the benefit of those with whom you work. We invite you to continue this narrative by sharing your story with us on www.eari.ie

# Bibliography

Ames, C. (1992), 'Classrooms: Goals, Structures, and Student Motivation', *Educational Psychology*, 84 (3): 261–71.

Apple, M. W. (1996), *Cultural Politics and Education*, Buckingham: Open University Press.

Apple, M. and J. Beane, eds (1999), *Democratic Schools: Lessons from the Chalk Face*, Buckingham: Open University Press.

Apte, J. (2009), 'Facilitating Transformative Learning: A Framework for Practice', *Australian Journal of Adult Learning*, 49 (1): 168–88.

Aronson, J., C. Fried and C. Good (2002), 'Reducing the Effects of Stereotype Threat on African American College Students by Shaping Theories of Intelligence', *Journal of Experimental Social Psychology*, 38: 113–25.

Atkinson, J. A. and N. T. Feather, eds (1966), *Theory of Achievement Motivation*, New York: John Wiley & Sons.

Aubussona, P., F. Steelea, S. Dinhamb and L. Bradyab (2007), 'Action Learning in Teacher Learning Community Formation: Informative or Transformative?' *Teacher Development*, 11 (2): 133–48.

Australian Institute for Teaching and School Leadership (AITSL) (2014), *Global Trends in Professional Learning and Performance & Development: Some Implications and Ideas for the Australian Education System*, Melbourne: AITSL.

Baker A. and S. Beames (2016), 'Good CoP: What Makes a Community of Practice Successful?' *Journal of Learning Design*, 9 (1): 72–9.

Ball, S. J. (2003), 'The Teacher's Soul and the Terrors of Performativity', *Journal of Education Policy*, 18 (2): 215–28.

Barak, J., A. Gidron and B. Turniansky (2010). 'Without Stones There Is No Arch: A Study of Professional Development of Teacher Educators as a Team', *Professional Development in Education*, 36 (1/2): 275–87.

Barth, R. (1990), *Improving Schools from Within*, San Francisco: Jossey Bass.

Bassey, M. (1999), *Case Study Research in Educational Settings*, Birmingham: Open University Press.

Beck, M., P. Howard and J. Long (1999), 'University and School Partnerships: Enhancing Tertiary Students' Learning', *HERDSA Annual International Conference*, Melbourne, 12–15 July.

Bezzina, C., P. Lorist and C. van Velzen (2006), 'Partnerships between Schools and Teacher Education Institutes', paper presented at 31st Annual ATEE Conference in Portoroz, Slovenia. 31st Annual ATEE conference proceedings: Association for Teacher Education in Europe, 747–58.

Bohm, D. (1996), *On Dialogue*, Available online: http://sprott.physics.wisc.edu/Chaos-Complexity/dialogue.pdf (accessed 31 October 2016).

Bohm, D. (2004), *On Dialogue*, Oxon: Routledge.

Bohm, D. and D. Peat (1987), *Science, Order, and Creativity*, New York: Bantam.

Bohm, D., D. Factor and P. Garrett (1991), 'Dialogue – a Proposal'. Available online: http://www.david-bohm.net/dialogue/dialogue_proposal.html#6 (accessed 12 July 2016).

Bolam, R., A. McMahon, L. Stoll, S. Thomas, M. Wallace, A. Greenwood, K. Hawkey, M. Ingram, A. Atkinson and M. Smith (2005), *Creating and Sustaining Effective Professional Learning Communities*, Research Report 637. London: DfES and University of Bristol.

Bolton, G. (2014), *Reflective Practice: Writing and Professional Development*, London: Sage.

Boniwell, I. (2012), *Positive Psychology in a Nutshell: The Science of Happiness*, Maidenhead, UK: McGraw-Hill Education.

Bornstein, J. C. (1991), 'Dialogue in the Classroom and the Community of Inquiry', in R. Reed (ed.), *When We Talk: Essays on Classroom Conversation*, Fort Worth: Analytic Teaching Press.

Brock, R. (2015), 'Intuition and Insight: Two Concepts That Illuminate the Tacit in Science Education', *Studies in Science Education*, 51 (2): 127–67.

Brodie, K. (2013), 'The Power of Professional Learning Communities', *Education as Change*, 17 (1): 5–18.

Brookfield, S. (1995), *Becoming a Critically Reflective Teacher*, San Francisco: Jossey-Bass.

Brookfield, S. (2009), 'The Concept of Critical Reflection: Promises and Contradictions', *European Journal of Social Work*, 12 (3): 293–304.

Brookfield, S. (2012), *Teaching for Critical Thinking: Tools and Techniques to Help Students Question Their Assumptions*, San Francisco: Jossey-Bass.

Brookfield, S. D. and S. Preskill (2005), *Discussion as a Way of Teaching: Tools and Techniques for Democratic Classrooms*, 2nd edn, San Francisco: Jossey-Bass.

Brydon-Miller, M., D. Greenwood and P. Maguire (2003), 'Why Action Research?', *Action Research*, 1 (1): 9–28.

Buber, M. (1958), *I and Thou*, 2nd edn, Edinburgh: T & T Clark.

Burbules, N. C. (1993), *Dialogue in Teaching: Theory and Practice*, New York: Teachers College Press.

Burbules, N. C. and S. Rice (1991), 'Dialogue across Differences: Continuing the Conversation', *Harvard Educational Review*, 61 (4): 393–416.

Capel, S., M. Leask and T. Turner (2009), *Learning to Teach in the Secondary School: A Companion to School Experience*, 5th edn, New York: Routledge.

Carr, W. and S. Kemmis (1986), *Becoming Critical: Education, Knowledge and Action Research*, London: Falmer Press.

*Children Full of Life* (2003), [Film] Dir. Noboru Kaetsu, Japan Broadcasting Corporation (NHK). Available online: http://kobreguide.com/children_full_of_life/ (accessed 16 August 2016).

Clark, C. M. (2001), *Talking Shop: Authentic Conversation and Teacher Learning*, New York: Teachers College Press.

Clarke, M. A. (1994), 'The Dysfunctions of the Theory/Practice Discourse', *TESOL Quarterly*, 28 (1): 9–26.

Clegg, S. R., M. Kornberger and C. Rhodes (2005), 'Learning/Becoming/Organizing', *Organization*, 12 (2): 147–67.

Cochran-Smith, M. and S. L. Lytle (1999), 'The Teacher Research Movement: A Decade Later', *Educational Researcher*, October: 15–23.

Cochran-Smith, M. and S. L. Lytle (2009a), 'Teacher Research as Stance', in S. Noffke and B. Somekh (eds), *The Sage Handbook of Educational Action Research*, 39–49, London: Sage.

Cochran-Smith, M. and S. L. Lytle (2009b), *Inquiry as Stance: Practitioner Research for the Next Generation*, New York: Teachers College Press.

Coghlan, D. and M. Brydon-Miller (2014), *The SAGE Encyclopedia of Action Research*, London: Sage.

Coghlan, D. and T. Brannick (2014), *Doing Action Research in Your Own Organisation*, 4th edn, London: Sage.

Collier, J. (1945), 'United States Indian Administration as a Laboratory of Ethnic Relations', *Social Research*, 12 (3), 265–303.

Conway, P. F., R. Murphy, A. Rath and K. Hall (2009), *Learning to Teach and Its Implications for the Continuum of Teacher Education: A Nine-Country Cross-National Study*, Cork: University College, Cork.

Cooperrider, D., D. D. Whitney and J. M. Stavros (2008), *The Appreciative Inquiry Handbook: For Leaders of Change*, 2nd edn, Ohio: Crown Custom.

Corey, S. M. (1953), *Action Research to Improve School Practices*, New York: Teachers College Press.

Csikszentmihalyi, M. (2002), *Flow: The Classic Work on How to Achieve Happiness*, London: Rider.

Dadds, M. (2001), 'The Politics of Pedagogy', *Teachers and Teaching: Theory and Practice*, 7 (1), 43–58.

Dadds, M. and S. Hart (2001), *Doing Practitioner Research Differently*, London: RoutledgeFalmer.

Danielson, C. (2016), *Talk about Teaching: Leading Professional Conversations*, Thousand Oaks, CA: Corwin.

Day, C. (1999), *Developing Teachers: The Challenges of Lifelong Learning*, London: Falmer.

Day, C. and J. Sachs (2004), 'Professionalism, Performativity and Empowerment: Discourses in the Politics, Policies and Purposes of Continuing Professional Development', in C. Day and J. Sachs (eds), *International Handbook on the Continuing Professional Development of Teachers*, 3–32, Berkshire: Open University Press.

Deverell, A. and S. Moore (2014), 'Releasing Creativity in Teaching and Learning: The Potential Role of Organisational Legitimacy and Increased Dialogue', *Innovations in Education & Teaching International*, 51 (2): 164–74.

Dewey, J. (1933), *How We Think: A Re-statement of the Relation of Reflective Thinking in the Educative Process*, Chicago: Henry Regnery.

Douglas, A. S. and V. Ellis (2011), 'Connecting Does Not Necessarily Mean Learning: Course Handbooks as Mediating Tools in School-University Partnerships', *Journal of Teacher Education*, 62 (5): 465–76.

DuFour, R. (2011), 'The Professional Learning Community (PLC) Continuum Rubric', Available online: http://collaborate.caedpartners.org/display/CAED/The+Professional+Learning+Community+%28PLC%29+Continuum+Rubric (accessed 1 August 2016).

Dweck, C. S. (1986), 'Motivational Processes Affecting Learning', *American Psychologist*, 41 (10): 1040–48.

Dweck, C. S. (2006), *Mindset: The New Psychology of Success*, New York: Ballantine Books.

Dweck, C. S. (2007), 'Boosting Achievement with Messages that Motivate', *Education Canada*, 47 (2): 6–10.

Dweck, C. S. (2012), *Mindset: How You Can Fulfil Your Potential* (reprint), London: Little, Brown Book Group.

Earle, S. (2014), 'Formative and Summative Assessment of Science in English Primary Schools: Evidence from the Primary Science Quality Mark', *Research in Science and Technological Education*, 32 (2): 216–28.

Earley, P. and V. Porritt, eds (2010), *Effective Practices in Continuing Professional Development: Lessons from Schools*, London: Institute of Education Press.

Elliott, J. (1998), *The Curriculum Experiment: Meeting the Challenge of Social Change*, Buckingham: Open University Press.

Elliott, J. (2000), 'Towards a Synoptic View of Educational Change in Advanced Industrial Societies', in H. Altrichter and J. Elliott (eds), *Images of Educational Change*, 175–220, Buckingham: Open University Press.

England, Department for Education (2012), *Teacher Appraisal and Capability: A Model Policy for Schools*. Available online: https://www.gov.uk/government/uploads/system/uploads/attachment_data/file/282598/Teacher_appraisal_and_capability.pdf (accessed 20 October 2016).

Eraut, M. (1994), *Developing Professional Knowledge and Competence*, London: Falmer Press.

Evans, L. (2008), 'Professionalism, Professionality and the Development of Education Professionals', *British Journal of Educational Studies*, 56 (1), 20–38.

Evans, R., E. Kurantowicz and E. Lucio-Villegas, eds (2016), *Researching and Transforming Adult Learning and Communities: The Local/Global Context*, Rotterdam: Sense.

Fancourt, N., A. Edwards and I. Menter (2015), 'Reimagining a School-University Partnership: The Development of the Oxford Education Deanery Narrative', *Education Inquiry*, 6 (3), September: 353–73.

Feiman-Nemser, S. (2001), 'From Preparation to Practice: Designing a Continuum to Strengthen and Sustain Teaching', *Teachers College Record*, 103 (6): 1015–55.

Fenton-O'Creevy, M., L. Brigham, S. Jones and A. Smith (2015), 'Students at the Academic-workplace Boundary: Tourists and Sojourners in Practice-based Education', in E. Wenger-Trayner, M. Fenton-O'Creevy, S. Hutchinson, C. Kubiak and B. Wenger-Trayner (eds), *Learning in Landscapes of Practice: Boundaries, Identity, and Knowledgeability in Practice-based Learning*, 13–29, London: Routledge.

Fenton-O'Creevy, M., Y. Dimitriadis and G. Scobie (2015), 'Failure and Resilience at Boundaries', in E. Wenger-Trayner, M. Fenton-O'Creevy, S. Hutchinson, C. Kubiak and B. Wenger-Trayner (eds), *Learning in Landscapes of Practice: Boundaries, Identity, and Knowledgeability in Practice-based Learning*, 33–42, London: Routledge.

Fitzallen, N. and N. Brown (2016), 'Turning Good Ideas into Quality Research', in S. Fan and J. Fielding-Wells (eds), *What Is Next in Educational Research?*, 3–10, Rotterdam: Sense.

Foucault, M. (1980a), 'The Eye of Power', in C. Gordon (ed.) *Power/Knowledge: Selected Interviews and Other Writings 1972–1977*, 146–65, Brighton: Harvester Press.

Foucault, M. (1980b), 'Truth and Power', in C. Gordon (ed.), *Power/ Knowledge: Selected Interviews and Other Writings 1972–1977*, 109–33, Brighton: Harvester Press.

Fox Eades, J. (2008), *Celebrating Strengths: Building Strengths-based Schools*, Coventry: CAPP Press.

Fredrickson, B. (2015), *Positivity: Groundbreaking Research to Release Your Inner Optimist and Thrive*, Oxford: Oneworld Publications.

Freire, P. (1970), *Pedagogy of the Oppressed*, New York: Seabury.

Freire, P. (2013), *Education for Critical Consciousness*, London: Bloomsbury Academic.

Fullan, M. (1993), *Change Forces: Probing the Depths of Educational Reform*, London: Falmer Press.

Gadamer, H. G. (1979), *Truth and Method*, London: Sheed and Ward.

Galvin, J., A. Higgins and K. Mahony (2009), *Family, School, Community Educational Partnership: Academic Report*, Limerick: Curriculum Development Unit, Mary Immaculate College.

Ganzach, Y., S. Keren, P. Asya and E. Dov (2016), 'The Joint Effect of Expectations and Performance on Efficacy Beliefs', *Personality and Individual Differences*, 88: 51–6.

Garet, M. S., A. C. Porter, L. Desimone, B. F. Birman and K. SukYoon (2001), 'What Makes Professional Development Effective? Results from a National Sample of Teachers', *American Educational Research Journal*, 38 (4): 915–45.

Garmston, R. J. and B. M. Wellman (1999), *The Adaptive School: A Sourcebook for Developing Collaborative Groups*, Norwood, MA: Christopher-Gordon.

Ghaye, A. and K. Ghaye (1998), *Teaching and Learning through Critical Reflective Practice*, London: David Fulton.

Giovanelli, M. (2015), 'Becoming an English Language Teacher: Linguistic Knowledge, Anxieties and the Shifting Sense of Identity', *Language and Education*, 29 (5): 416–29.

Giroux, H. (2011), *On Critical Pedagogy*, New York: Continuum.

Glassman, M. (2001), 'Dewey and Vygotsky: Society, Experience, and Inquiry in Educational Practice', *Educational Researcher*, 30 (4): 3–14.

Glenn, M. (2006), 'Working with Collaborative Projects: My Living Theory of a Holistic Educational Practice', unpublished PhD thesis, University of Limerick. Available online: http://www.eari.ie (accessed 28 July 2016).

Glenn, M., C. McDonagh, B. Sullivan, M. Roche, with M. Morgan (2012), *Practice-based Research Encompassing Professional Development Project: Final report March 2012*. Available online: http://www.eari.ie/research-and-publications/ (accessed 21 September 2016).

Glenn, M., B. Sullivan, C. McDonagh and M. Roche (2012), 'Communities: Partnerships in Action'. Presentation to Hibernia College School Partnership Conference, Dublin, 30 November.

Goldie, J. (2012), 'The Formation of Professional Identity in Medical Students: Considerations for Educators', *Medical Teacher*, 34 (9): 641–8.

Good, C., J. Aronson and M. Inzlicht (2003), 'Improving Adolescents' Standardized Test Performance: An Intervention to Reduce the Effects of Stereotype Threat', *Journal of Applied Developmental Psychology*, 24: 645–62.

Goodlad, J. (1984), *A Place Called School: Prospects for the Future*, New York: McGraw-Hill Book.

Government of Ireland (2015), 'Measuring Teacher Effectiveness in Ireland and Internationally', in *Supporting Teachers and Enhancing Teacher Effectiveness*, Houses of the Oireachtas: Library and Research Service. (*L&RS Note*).

Greany, T. and C. Brown (2015), *Partnerships between Teaching Schools and Universities: Research Report*, London: London Centre for Leadership in Learning, UCL Institute of Education, March.

Greany, T., Qing Gu, G. Handscomb, with M. Manners and S. Duncan (2014), *School–University Partnerships: Fulfilling the Potential Summary Report*. National Co-ordinating Centre for Public Engagement, Research Council, UK.

Gredler, M. and C. Shields (2004), 'Does No One Read Vygotsky's Words? Commentary on Glassman', *Educational Researcher*, 33 (2): 21–5.

Groundwater-Smith, S., C. E. Deer, H. Sharp and P. March (1997), 'The Practicum as Workplace Learning: A Multimode Approach in Teacher Education', *Australian Journal of Teacher Education*, 21 (2): 21–9.

Haggerty, L. (2004), 'An Alternative Vision for the Thoughtful Teacher', *British Educational Research Journal*, 30 (4): 591–600.

Hairona, S. and Dimmock, C. (2014), 'Singapore Schools and Professional Learning Communities: Teacher Professional Development and School Leadership in an Asian Hierarchical System', *Educational Review*, 64 (4): 405–24.

Hall, B. L. (2016), 'Towards a Knowledge Democracy Movement', in R. Evans, E. Kurantowicz and E. Lucio-Villegas (eds), *Researching and Transforming Adult Learning and Communities: The Local/Global Context*, 15–26, Rotterdam: Sense.

Hamilton, M. L. and S. Pinnegar (1998), 'The Value and the Promise of Self-study', in M. L. Hamilton (ed.), *Reconceptualising Teaching Practice: Self-Study in Teacher Education*, 235–46, London: Falmer Press.

Hanh, T. N. (1995), *Living Buddha, Living Christ*, New York: Riverhead Books.

Hargreaves, A. (1992), 'Cultures of Teaching: A Focus for Change', in A. Hargreaves and M. Fullan (eds), *Understanding Teacher Development*, 216–40, New York: Teachers College Press.

Hargreaves, A. (2003), *Teaching in the Knowledge Society: Education in the Age of Insecurity*, Maidenhead: Open University Press.

Hargreaves, E. (2013), 'Assessment for Learning and Teacher Learning Communities: UK Teachers' Experiences', *Teacher Education*, 24 (3): 327–44.

Harris, D. N. and T. R. Sass (2008), 'Teacher Training, Teacher Quality, and Student Achievement', *National Centre for Analysis of Longitudinal Data in Education Research, Working Paper 3*. Available online: http://www.caldercenter.org/sites/default/files/1001059_Teacher_Training.pdf

Healey, M., A. Flint and K. Harrington (2014), *Engagement through Partnership: Students as Partners in Learning and Teaching in Higher Education*, York: The Higher Education Academy.

Hiebert, J., R. Gallimore and J. W. Stigler (2002), 'A Knowledge Base for the Teaching Profession: What Would It Look Like and How Can We Get One?', *Educational Researcher*, 31 (5): 3–15.

Hislop, H. (2013), 'Applying an Evaluation and Assessment Framework: An Irish Perspective', Irish Presidency of the Council of the European Union, Presidency Conference: Better Assessment and Evaluation to Improve Teaching and Learning, Dublin Castle, Ireland.

hooks, b. (1994), *Teaching to Transgress: Education as the Practice of Freedom*, New York: Routledge.

Hoyle, E. (1975), 'Professionality, Professionalism and Control in Teaching', in V. Houghton, R. McHugh and C. Morgan (eds), *Management in Education: The Management of Organisations and Individuals*, London: Ward Lock Educational in association with Open University Press.

Humada-Ludeke, A. (2013), *The Creation of a Professional Learning Community for School Leaders: Insights on the Change Process from the Lens of the School Leader*, Rotterdam: Sense.

Illeris, K. (2002), *Three Dimensions of Learning: Contemporary Learning Theory in the Tension Field between the Cognitive, the Emotional and the Social*, Denmark: Roskilde University Press.

Ireland, Department of Education and Skills (2011), *Literacy and Numeracy for Learning and Life: The National Strategy to Improve Literacy and Numeracy among Children and Young People 2011–2020*, Dublin: Stationery Office.

Ireland, Department of Education and Skills (2012a), *School Self-Evaluation: Guidelines for Primary Schools*, Dublin: Stationery Office.

Ireland, Department of Education and Skills (2012b), *School Self-Evaluation Guidelines for Post-Primary Schools*, Dublin: Stationery Office.

Ireland, Department of Education and Skills (2016a), *Looking at Our School 2016: A Quality Framework for Primary Schools*, Dublin Department of Education and Skills.

Ireland, Department of Education and Skills (2016b), *Looking at Our School 2016: A Quality Framework for Post-Primary Schools*, Dublin: Department of Education and Skills.

Jenkins, A., R. Breen, R. Lindsay and A. Brew (2003), *Reshaping Teaching in Higher Education: Linking Teaching and Research*, London: Routledge.

Kadi-Hanifi, K. (2010), 'Teachers as Theorists', *International Journal of Learning and Change*, 4 (3): 206–16.

Kalmbach Phillips, D. and K. Carr (2010), *Becoming a Teacher through Action Research*, 2nd edn, London and New York: Routledge.

Kincheloe, J. L. (2003), *Teachers as Researchers: Qualitative Inquiry as a Path to Empowerment*, 2nd edn, London: Routledge.

King, F. (2014), 'Evaluating the Impact of Teacher Professional Development: An Evidence Based Framework', *Professional Development in Education*, 40 (1): 89–111.

Kitching, K., M. Morgan and M. O'Leary (2009), 'It's the Little Things: Exploring the Importance of Commonplace Events for Early-Career Teachers' Motivation', *Teachers and Teaching: Theory and Practice*, 15 (1): 43–58.

Kooy, M. (2015), 'Building a Teacher–Student Community through Collaborative Teaching and Learning: Engaging the Most Affected and Least Consulted', *Teacher Development*, 19 (2): 187–209.

Krovetz, M. L. (1993), 'Collegial Learning Communities: The Road to School Restructuring School', *The School Community Journal*, 3 (2): 71–82.

Lalande, M. A. (2012), 'What Is a PLN – Marc-André Lalande's Take'. Available online: https://youtu.be/hLLpWqp-owo (accessed 7 July 2016).

Lave, J. and E. Wenger (1991), *Situated Learning: Legitimate Peripheral Participation*, Cambridge: Cambridge University Press.

Leonard, L. and P. Leonard (2003), 'Valuing Schools as Professional Communities: Assessing the Collaborative Prescription', in P. Begley and J.

Olaf (eds), *The Ethical Dimensions of School Leadership*, 127–42, Boston, MA: Kluwer Academic.

Lewin, K. (1946), 'Action Research and Minority Problems', *Journal of Social Issues*, 2 (4): 34–46.

Lewis, D. and B. Allan (2005), *Virtual Learning Communities: A Guide for Practitioners*, Maidenhead: Open University Press.

Lieberman, A., ed. (1988), *Building a Professional Culture in Schools*, New York: Teachers College Press.

Lingard, B. and P. Renshaw (2010), 'Teaching as a Research-Informed and Research-Informing Profession', in A. Campbell and S. Groundwater-Smith (eds), *Connecting Inquiry and Professional Learning in Education*, 26–39, London: Routledge.

Livingston, K. (2012), 'Quality in Teachers' Professional Career-Long Development', in J. Harford, B. Hudson and H. Niemi (eds), *Quality Assurance and Teacher Education: International Challenges and Expectations*, 35–51, Oxford: Peter Lang.

Lortie, D. (1975), *Schoolteacher: A Sociological Study*, London: University of Chicago Press.

Loughran, J. (2002), 'Understanding Self-Study of Teacher Education Practices', in J. Loughran and T. Russell (eds), *Improving Teacher Education Practices through Self-Study*, 239–48, London and New York: RoutledgeFalmer.

Lowenthal, P. and R. Muth (2008), 'Constructivism', in E. F. Provenzo, Jr. (ed.), *Encyclopedia of the Social and Cultural Foundations of Education*, Thousand Oaks, CA: Sage.

MacLure, M. (1996), 'Telling Transitions: Boundary Work in Narratives of Becoming an Action Researcher', *British Educational Research Journal*, 22 (3): 273–83.

Mattsson, M., T. Vidar Eilertsen and D. Rorrison (eds) (2011), *A Practicum Turn in Teacher Education*. Pedagogy, Education and Praxis, Vol 6, Rotterdam: Sense.

May, S. (ed.) (1999), *Indigenous Community-Based Education*, Clevedon: Multilingual Matters.

McAuslan, F. and P. Nicholson (2010), *The Resolving Bereavement Book*, Dublin, Ireland: Veritas.

McDermott, R. P. (1999), 'On Becoming Labelled – the Story of Adam', in P. Murphy (ed.), *Learners, Learning and Assessment*, 1–22, London: Paul Chapman.

McDonagh, C. (2007), 'My Living Theory of Learning to Teach for Social Justice: How Do I Enable Primary School Children with Specific Learning Disability (Dyslexia) and Myself as Their Teacher to Realise Our Learning Potentials?', unpublished PhD thesis, University of Limerick. Available online: http://www.eari.ie (accessed 27 July 2016).

McDonagh, C., M. Roche, B. Sullivan and M. Glenn (2012), *Enhancing Practice through Classroom Research: A Teacher's Guide to Professional Development*, Abingdon: Routledge.

McLaren, P. (1999), 'A Pedagogy of Possibility: Reflecting upon Paulo Freire's Politics of Education', *Educational Researcher*, March, 49–54.

McLaren, P. (2003), 'Critical Pedagogy: A Look at the Major Concepts', in A. Darder, M. Baltodano and R. D. Torres (eds), *The Critical Pedagogy Reader*, 69–96, New York: RoutledgeFalmer.

McLaren, P. (2015), *Pedagogy of Insurrection: From Resurrection to Revolution*, New York: Peter Lang.

McLaren, P. and T. T. DaSilva (1993), 'Decentering Pedagogy: Critical Literacy, Resistance and the Politics of Memory', in P. McLaren and P. Leonard (eds), *Paulo Freire: A Critical Encounter*, London: Routledge, 47–89.

McNiff, J. (1993), *Teaching as Learning: An Action Research Approach*, London: Routledge.

McNiff, J. (2010), *Action Research for Professional Development: Concise Advice for New and Experienced Action Researchers*, Poole, UK: September Books.

McNiff, J. (2013), *Action Research: Principles and Practice*, 3rd edn, London: Routledge.

McNiff, J. (2015), *Writing Up Your Action Research Project*, Abingdon: Routledge.

McNiff, J. and J. Whitehead (2005), *Action Research for Teachers: A Practical Guide*, London: David Fulton.

McNiff, J. and J. Whitehead (2009), *Doing and Writing Action Research*, London: Sage.

Montessori, M. (1949), *The Absorbent Mind*, Madras, India: Theosophical Publishing House.

Morehouse, R. (1991), 'Conversation and Cognition', in R. Reed (ed.), *When We Talk: Essays on Classroom Conversation*, 97–113, Fort Worth: Analytic Teaching Press.

Morgan M., L. Ludlow, K. Kitching, M. O'Leary and A. Clarke (2010), 'What Makes Teachers Tick? Sustaining Events in New Teachers' Lives', *British Educational Research Journal*, 36 (2): 191–208.

National Council for Curriculum and Assessment (NCCA) (2007), *Assessment in the Primary School*. Available at: http://www.ncca.ie/en/Curriculum_and_Assessment/.

Nias, J. (1989), *Primary Teachers Talking: A Study of Teaching as Work*, London: Routledge.

Niemi, H., J. Harford and B. Hudson (2012), 'Introduction: From Quality Assurance to Quality Culture', in J. Harford, B. Hudson and H. Niemi (eds), *Quality Assurance and Teacher Education: International Challenges and Expectations*, 1–11, Bern: Peter Lang.

Noddings, N. (1992), *The Challenge to Care in Schools: An Alternative Approach to Education*, New York: Teachers College.

Noffke. S. (2009), 'Revisiting the Professional, Personal and Political Dimensions of Action Research', in S. Noffke and B. Somekh (eds), *The Sage Handbook of Educational Action Research*, 6–24, London: Sage.

Norris, J. M. and M. Seligman (2015), *Positive Education: The Geelong Grammar School Journey*, Oxford: Oxford University Press.

Northern Ireland, Department of Education (2010), *The Teacher Education Partnership Handbook*. Available online: https://www.education-ni.gov.uk/articles/teacher-education-partnership-handbook (accessed 30 October 2016).

O'Brien, L. M. (2002), 'A Response to "Dewey and Vygotsky: Society, Experience, and Inquiry in Educational Practice"', *Educational Researcher*, 31 (5): 21–3.

O'Doherty, T. and J. Deegan (2009), 'Mentors, Not Models: Supporting Teachers to Be Empowered in an Irish Context', *Research in Comparative and International Education*, 4 (1): 22–33.

O'Donohue, J. (2003), *Divine Beauty: The Invisible Embrace*, London: Transworld.

OECD (2005), *Teachers Matter: Attracting, Developing and Retaining Effective Teachers*, Paris: OECD.

OECD (2013), 'Improving Teaching Using Appraisal and Feedback', TALIS 2013 *Results, Chapter 5,* Paris: OECD.

Office for Standards in Education (OFSTED) (2006), *The Logical Chain: Continuing Professional Development in Effective Schools.* London: Crown. Available online: www.ofsted.gov.uk.

O'Hanlon, C. (2002), 'Reflection and Action in Research: Is There a Moral Responsibility to Act?', in C. Day, J. Elliott, B. Somekh and R. Winter (eds), *Theory and Action in Action Research*, 111–20, Oxford: Symposium Books.

Ong'ondo, C. O. and Jwan, J. O. (2009), 'Research on Student Teacher Learning, Collaboration and Supervision during the Practicum: A Literature Review', *Educational Research and Review*, 4 (11): 515–24.

Owen, S. (2014), 'Teacher Professional Learning Communities: Going beyond Contrived Collegiality toward Challenging Debate and Collegial Learning and Professional Growth', *Australian Journal of Adult Learning*, 54 (2): 54–76.

Palmer, P. (1997), *The Courage to Teach: Exploring the Inner Landscape of a Teacher's Life*, San Francisco: Jossey-Bass.

Palmer, P., 'The Heart of a Teacher Identity and Integrity in Teaching'. Available online: http://www.couragerenewal.org/PDFs/Parker-Palmer_The-Heart-of-a-Teacher.pdf (accessed 21 September 2016).

Paraskeva, J. M. (2015), 'Introduction – Let's Begin at the Beginning', in J. M. Paraskeva and T. LaVallee (eds), *Transformative Researchers and Educators for Democracy: Dartmouth Dialogues*, vii–xxix, Rotterdam: Sense.

Pockett, R. and R. Giles (2008), *Critical Reflection: Generating Theory from Practice: The Graduating Social Work Student Experience*, Sydney: Darlington Press.

Polanyi, M. (1958), *Personal Knowledge*, London: Routledge and Keegan Paul.

Prawat, R. S. (2002), 'Dewey and Vygotsky Viewed through the Rearview Mirror – and Dimly at That', *Educational Researcher*, 31 (5): 16–20.

Reason, P. and H. Bradbury (2013), *The SAGE Handbook of Action Research: Participative Inquiry and Practice*, 3rd edn, London: Sage.

Rivkin, S. G., F. A. Hanushek and J. F. Kain (2005), 'Teachers, Schools and Academic Achievement', *Econometrica*, 73 (2): 417–58.

Roche, M. (2007), 'Towards a Living Theory of Caring Pedagogy: Interrogating My Practice to Nurture a Critical, Emancipatory and Just Community of Enquiry', unpublished PhD thesis, University of Limerick. Available online: http://www.,eari.ie (accessed 27 July 2016).

Roche, M. (2011), 'Creating a Dialogical and Critical Classroom: Reflection and Action to Improve Practice', *Educational Action Research*, 19 (3), 327–43.

Roche, M. (2014), 'Developing Researcherly Dispositions in an Initial Teacher Education Context: Successes and Dilemmas', *International Journal for Transformative Research*, 1 (1), September (de Gruyter): 45–63.

Roche, M. (2015), *Developing Children's Critical Thinking through Picturebooks*, Abingdon: Routledge.

Roche, M., C. McDonagh, B. Sullivan and M. Glenn (2010), 'Communities of Learning and Professional Development', presentation to Irish National

Teachers Organisation 25th Annual Consultative Conference on Education, November 19–30.

Rorrison, D. (2011), 'Border Crossing in Practicum Research: Reframing How We Talk about Practicum Learning', in M. Mattsson, T. Vidar Eilertsen and D. Rorrison (eds), *A Practicum Turn in Teacher Education*, 19–45. *Pedagogy, Education and Praxis*, Vol 6, Rotterdam: Sense.

Roth, G. L. and A. Kleiner (1998), 'Developing Organisational Memory through Learning Histories', *Organisational Dynamics*, 27 (2): 43–60.

Russell, T. (2002), 'Guiding New Teachers' Learning from Classroom Experience: Self-Study of the Faculty Liaison Role', in Loughran, J. and T. Russell (eds), *Improving Teacher Education Practices through Self-Study*, 73–87, London and New York: RoutledgeFalmer.

Ryan, R. M. and E. L. Deci (2000), 'Self-Determination Theory and the Facilitation of Intrinsic Motivation, Social Development, and Well-Being', *American Psychologist*, 55 (1), 68–78.

Sachs, J. (2005), *The Activist Teaching Profession*, Buckingham: Open University Press.

Savin-Baden, M. and C. H. Major (2004), *Foundations of Problem-Based Learning*, Maidenhead: Open University Press.

Scaife, J. (2009), *Supervision in Clinical Practice: A Practitioner's Guide*, Hove: Routledge.

Schön, D. A. (1983), *The Reflective Practitioner: How Professionals Think in Action*, New York: Basic Books.

Schön, D. A. (1995), 'Knowing-in-Action: The New Knowledge Requires a New Epistemology', *Change*, November/December, 27–34.

Scottish Executive (2005), *Review of Initial Teacher Education Stage 2: Report of the Review Group* (Edinburgh: 2005).

Seashore, K. R., A. R. Anderson and E. Riedel (2003), *Implementing Arts for Academic Achievement: The Impact of Mental Models, Professional Community and Interdisciplinary Teaming*. Paper presented at the Seventeenth Conference of the International Congress for School Effectiveness and Improvement, Rotterdam, January.

Seligman, M. E. P. (2003), *Authentic Happiness*, London: Nicholas Brealey.

Seligman, M. E. P. and M. Csikszentmihalyi (2000), 'Positive Psychology: An Introduction'. *American Psychologist*, 55 (1) : 5–14.

Seligman, M. E. P., M. Randal, E. J. Gillhamc, K. Reivicha and M. Linkinsd (2009), 'Positive Education: Positive Psychology and Classroom Interventions', *Oxford Review of Education*, 35 (3): 293–311.

Senge, P., A. Kleiner, C. Roberts, R. Ross and B. Smith (1994), *The Fifth Discipline Fieldbook: Strategies and Tools for Building a Learning Organization*, New York: Bantam Doubleday Dell.

Sergiovanni, T. S. (1994), *Building Community in Schools*, San Francisco: Jossey-Bass.

Shulman, L. S. (1999), 'Taking Learning Seriously', *Change*, 31 (4): 10–17.

Sjoer, E and J. Meirink (2016), 'Understanding the Complexity of Teacher Interaction in a Teacher Professional Learning Community', *European Journal of Teacher Education*, 39 (1): 110–25.

Somekh, B. and S. Noffke (eds) (2009), *The SAGE Handbook of Educational Action Research*, London: Sage.

Spivak, G. C. (1988), *In Other Worlds: Essays in Cultural Politics*, New York: Routledge.

Stenhouse, L. (1975), *An Introduction to Curriculum Research and Development*, London: Heinemann.

Stiggins, R. (2004), 'New Assessment Beliefs for a New School Mission', *Phi Delta Kappan*, 86 (1): 22–7.

Stoll, L., R. Bolam, A. McMahon, M. Wallace and S. Thomas (2006), 'Professional Learning Communities: A Review of the Literature', *Journal of Educational Change*, 7 (4): 221–58.

Sugrue, C. (1998), 'Confronting Student Teachers' Lay Theories and Culturally Embedded Archetypes of Teaching', in C. Sugrue (ed.), *Teaching, Curriculum and Educational Research*, 118–41, Dublin: St. Patrick's College.

Sugrue, C., M. Morgan, D. Devine and D. Rafferty (2001), *The Quality of Professional Learning for Irish Primary and Secondary Teachers: A Critical Analysis*, Dublin: Department of Education and Science.

Sullivan, B. (2006), 'A Living Theory of a Practice of Social Justice: Realising the Right of Traveller Children to Educational Equality', unpublished PhD thesis, University of Limerick. Available online: http://www.eari.ie (accessed 28 July 2016).

Sullivan, B., M. Glenn, M. Roche and C. McDonagh (2016), *Introduction to Critical Reflection and Action for Teacher Researchers*, London: Routledge.

Tannehill, D. and A. MacPhail (2016), 'Teacher Empowerment through Engagement in a Learning Community in Ireland: Working across Disadvantaged Schools', *Professional Development in Education*. Available online: http://www.tandfonline.com/doi/abs/10.1080/19415257.2016.1183508 (accessed 4 October 2016).

Teaching Council of Ireland (2012a), *Practice-Based Research Encompassing Professional Development Project*, available online: http://www.teachingcouncil.ie/en/Publications/Research/Documents/Practice-based-Research-Encompassing-Professional-Development-Project.pdf (accessed 21 June 2016).

Teaching Council of Ireland (2012b), *The Code of Professional Conduct for Teachers*, 2nd edn, Maynooth: Teaching Council.

Teaching Council of Ireland (2013), *Teacher Education: Guidelines for School Placement*, Maynooth: Teaching Council.

Teaching Council of Ireland (2016), *The Code of Professional Conduct for Teachers*, 2nd edn, Maynooth: Teaching Council.

Teaching Council of Ireland (2017), *Droichead: An Integrated Framework for Newly Qualified Teachers*, revised edn, Maynooth: Teaching Council.

UK, Department for Education and Skills (2004), *A New Relationship with Schools: Improving Performance through School Self-Evaluation*, Nottingham: DfES Publications.

Vygotsky, L. S. (1978), *Mind in Society: The Development of Higher Psychological Processes*, Cambridge, MA: Harvard University Press.

Wakefield, P. (2001), 'A Philosophy of Assessment', *Assessment Update: Progress, Trends, and Practices in Higher Education*, 13 (2): 6–7.

Walsh, T. (2016), 'Súile ar an gCosán: Irish Primary School Teachers' views on CPD', paper presented at *Education Studies Association of Ireland Conference Galway*, 2 April.

Watson, C. (2014), 'Effective Professional Learning Communities? The Possibilities for Teachers as Agents of Change in Schools', *British Educational Research Journal*, 40 (1), 18–29.

Weiner, B. (1985), 'An Attributional Theory of Achievement Motivation and Emotion', *Psychological Review*, 92 (4): 548–73.

Weissenrieder, J., B. Roesken-winter, S, Schueler, E. Binner and S. Blömeke (2015), 'Scaling CPD through Professional Learning Communities: Development of Teachers' Self-Efficacy in Relation to Collaboration', *ZD*, 47 (1), 27–38.

Wenger, E. (1998), *Communities of Practice: Learning, Meaning and Identity*, Cambridge: Cambridge University Press.

Wenger-Trayner, E. and B. Wenger-Trayner (2015), 'Learning in a Landscape of Practice', in E. Wenger-Trayner, M. Fenton-O'Creevy, S. Hutchinson, C. Kubiak, C. and B. Wenger-Trayner (eds), *Learning in Landscapes of Practice: Boundaries, Identity, and Knowledgeability in Practice-Based Learning*, 13–29, London: Routledge.

Whitaker, T., J. Zoul and J. Casas (2015), *What Connected Educators Do Differently*, New York: Routledge.

Whitehead, J. (1989), 'Creating a Living Educational Theory from Questions of the Kind, "How Do I Improve My Practice?"', *Cambridge Journal of Education*, 19 (1), 137–53.

Whitehead, J. (1993), *The Growth of Educational Knowledge: Creating Your Own Living Educational Theories*, Bournemouth: Hyde.

Whitehead, J. (2000), 'How Do I Improve My Practice? Creating and Legitimating an Epistemology of Practice', *Reflective Practice*, 1 (1): 91–104.

Whitehead, J. (2013), 'Research and Practice', A keynote presentation to the Sixth International Conference on Teacher Education on Changing Reality through Education, MOFET Institute, Tel Aviv, 4 July.

Whitehead, J. (2015), 'The Practice of Helping Students Find Their First Person Voice in Creating Living Theories for Education', in H. Bradbury (ed.), *The Sage Handbook of Action Research*, 3rd edn, 246–54, London and Thousand Oaks, CA: Sage.

Whitehead, J. (2016), 'Jack Whitehead Presents at NEARI'. Available online: http://eariblog.edublogs.org/2016/02/11/jack-whitehead-presents-at-neari/ (accessed 1 August 2016).

Whitehead J. and J. McNiff (2006), *Action Research: Living Theory*, London: Sage.

Wiles, F. F. (2013), '"Not Easily Put Into a Box": Constructing Professional Identity', *Social Work Education*, 32 (7): 854–66.

Winter, R. and C. Munn-Giddings (2001), *A Handbook for Action Research in Health and Social Care*, London: Routledge.

Wolters, C. A., W. Fan and S. G. Dougherty (2013), 'Examining Achievement Goals and Causal Attributions Together as Predictors of Academic Functioning', *Journal of Experimental Education*, 81 (3): 295–321.

Wong, E. (2008), 'Explication of Tacit Knowledge in Higher Education Institutional Research through the Criteria of Professional Practice Action Research Approach: A Focus Group Case Study at an Australian University', *International Journal of Doctoral Studies*, 3: 43–58.

Ya-Ni, A. (2013), 'Comparing the Effectiveness of Classroom and Online Learning: Teaching Research Methods', *Journal of Public Affairs Education*, 19 (2): 199–215, Spring.

Yoshida, A. (2002), 'Martin Buber, Education as Holistic Encounter and Dialogue', in J. Miller and Y. Nakagawa (eds), *Nurturing Our Wholeness: Perspectives on Spirituality in Education*, Brandon, VT: Foundation for Educational Renewal.

Zeichner, K. (2010), 'Rethinking the Connections between Campus Courses and Field Experiences in College- and University-Based Teacher Education', *Journal of Teacher Education*, 61 (1–2): 89–99.

Zeichner, K. (2015), 'How Teacher Education Can Contribute to Social Transformation and Greater Justice', keynote address, SCoTENS conference, *Teacher Education for Social Justice*, Limerick: Strand Hotel, 15–16 October.

Zhao, Ying (2011), 'Professional Learning Community and College English Teachers' Professional Development', *Journal of Language Teaching and Research*, 4 (6): 1365–70.

# Index